ADVANCE PRAISE FOR
JUDAISM WITHOUT TRIBALISM

"Shapiro's powerful manifesto is a timely and valuable roadmap for an age fraught with ideological division, hatred, and violence. It offers contemplative thought-starters and practical advice for how to invent a better future for all people in the human family."
—*Spirituality & Health Magazine*

"*Judaism Without Tribalism* is a blessing, a much-needed challenge, and a deep well of wisdom and sanity."
—Natalie Goldberg, author of the bestselling *Writing Down the Bones* and *Three Simple Lines*

"An influential religious leader confronts Jewish tribalism in this spiritual guide...Orthodox Jews [may], of course, bristle at the work's progressive spirituality, universalization of Judaism, and critiques of tradition. But the book succeeds in its mission to 'make Judaism accessible to everyone' by providing a Jewish lens that could be of use in the spiritual journeys of Jews and non-Jews alike. A compelling, progressive reorientation of an ancient faith."
—*Kirkus Reviews*

"Easy to read, yet deep and challenging in its wisdom, this book will become a bible for many who have rejected various Jewish orthodoxies but still know that there is a depth of wisdom in Judaism that they do not want to discard."
—Rabbi Michael Lerner, editor of *Tikkun Magazine* and author of the bestselling *The Left Hand of God* and *Jewish Renewal*

"In *Judaism Without Tribalism*, Rabbi Rami brings us the revolutionary essence of the Jewish path, fearlessly smashing the dull idols we have accrued along the way. Rami is an iconoclast extraordinaire, with the moxie to call out religious deceptions that keep us stuck in darkness, and the spiritual clarity to illuminate the jewels of wisdom that can help us change our lives for good. This book is like fresh rain on parched soil."

—Rabbi Tirzah Firestone, PhD, author of *Wounds Into Wisdom: Healing Intergenerational Jewish Trauma*

"Rami Shapiro calls on us to question authorities of our time, within Jewish life and in our broader world, identifying the sacred precisely in what others see as 'strange.'"

—Dan Libenson and Lex Rofeberg, co-hosts of the *Judaism Unbound* podcast

"*Judaism Without Tribalism* is the best book I ever read. I say that every time Rabbi Rami writes a new book—and it's absolutely true. He is a master teacher full of love, wisdom and a reverent irreverence that illuminates both mind and heart."

—Dr. Joan Borysenko, author of the bestselling *Pocketful of Miracles*

"Rabbi Rami is a great mystical teacher."

—Andrew Harvey, author of *The Direct Path*

"Rabbi Rami fuses intellect, passion, and humor in a beautiful and powerful way that radiates truth."

—Wayne Teasdale, author of *The Mystic Heart*

JUDAISM
WITHOUT
TRIBALISM

A Guide to Being a Blessing
to All the Peoples of the Earth

Rabbi Rami Shapiro
INTRODUCTION BY DOUGLAS RUSHKOFF

Monkfish Book Publishing Company
Rhinebeck, New York

Judaism Without Tribalism: A Guide to Being a Blessing to All the Peoples of the Earth
© 2022 by Rabbi Rami Shapiro

Paperback ISBN 978-1-948626-65-1
eBook ISBN 978-1-948626-66-8

Library of Congress Cataloging-in-Publication Data

Names: Shapiro, Rami M., author.
Title: Judaism without tribalism : a guide to being a blessing to all the
  peoples of the earth / Rabbi Rami Shapiro ; introduction by Douglas
  Rushkoff.
Description: Rhinebeck, New York : Monkfish Book Publishing Company, [2022]
Identifiers: LCCN 2021061077 (print) | LCCN 2021061078 (ebook) | ISBN
  9781948626651 (paperback) | ISBN 9781948626668 (ebook)
Subjects: LCSH: Judaism. | Jewish way of life.
Classification: LCC BM45 .S4618 2022 (print) | LCC BM45 (ebook) | DDC
  296--dc23/eng/20211223
LC record available at https://lccn.loc.gov/2021061077
LC ebook record available at https://lccn.loc.gov/2021061078

Book and cover design by Colin Rolfe
"Minimal Eucalyptis Leaves" photo by Annie Spratt on Unsplash

Monkfish Book Publishing Company
22 East Market Street, Suite 304
Rhinebeck, NY 12572
(845) 876-4861
monkfishpublishing.com

CONTENTS

FOREWORD

For many people, I suspect, Judaism without tribalism won't sound like Judaism at all. That's because Judaism—at least as my friend Rami Shapiro and I understand it—may best be thought of less as a religion than the way we get over religion.

Think about it. Our Torah doesn't tell the story of the founding of a religion. It's about our escape from an empire of slaves controlled by death cults. We are rescued from Egypt, or *mitzrayim*—not just "the narrow place" imprisoning Israelite bodies, but a narrow mindset imprisoning Israelite hearts and souls.

And how do we get out of there? The plagues, each of which represents the desecration of another Egyptian god. Blood desecrates the Nile, a god. Locusts desecrate the corn god, and so on, until we get to the ultimate desecration. In April, the Egyptian New Year, when everyone is supposed to be worshipping a ram, what do the Israelites do? Kill a lamb as a sacrifice—an abomination in Egypt—and then put the blood on the door, as if to publicize the fact.

Out to the desert we run. For forty years we walk around out there, not to create a new religion but to wean ourselves off the need for idols, and beliefs, and any religiosity at all. The whole generation of "believers" has to die off. Sure, we build an Ark of the Covenant, and it's pretty much like the Egyptian arks we built before as slaves. But there's one key difference: there's no god up on the top. Rather, there's an empty space guarded by two fierce cherubs. We get no "thing" to worship, and those cherubs are going to make certain of it.

Sure, occasionally we go crazy and try to shove something into that empty space. Moses can't turn his back for a minute before we're crafting a golden calf of one kind or another. And even today, we try to deify silly things like money and power, or even important things like education or Israel. But none of them are gods.

No, our deity is so unknowable, unseeable, unnamable that it may as well not be there at all. That may be the whole point. Judaism invites us to take our gaze off the idealized icon in the sky—however temporarily reassuring—and place it on one another.

Yes, we are the real prize, here. We people. Our families, communities, friends, neighbors—and even those people over there who we don't quite understand and certainly don't agree with.

Living in a tradition like this, as Tevye reminded us, isn't easy. It requires constant improvisation and adaptation to new circumstances, grounded only in the wisdom of the generations that preceded us. Our Talmudic laws may be helpful guideposts, but our morality comes in the moment, spontaneously emerging from our conscience. And this conscience, this moral sensibility, is what we learn from our stories, our community, our experiences, our holidays, and our parents.

Judaism without tribalism requires us to abandon the idols and icons, brands and beliefs on which we might prefer to rely as we navigate a course through the strange, modern world. But these symbols are not up to the challenge. They're dead, static traps—artifacts of fear and desire—and not at all relevant to lived experience of Jewishness.

I've always found it telling that the five books of Torah—the first and most sacred books of the Bible—end before the Israelites make it into Canaan. The story leaves them in the desert, as if to make sure we understand that this is the truest and most essential state of being for a Jew. In between here and there, this and that, the narrow place and the promised land. Always in between, always in motion, always alive, and—if we do it right—always in love.

With love,
Douglas Rushkoff
New York City

TRIBE AND TRIBALISM

Tribe: An aggregate of people united by a shared story.

*

Tribalism: Mistaking story as history in service to the elevation of one tribe over all others.

*

Jewish tribalism: The belief that there is one god, creator of heaven and earth, who chose the Jews from among all peoples to be the recipients of his (sic) one and only revelation (Torah), and to hold the deed to the Promised Land in perpetuity.

*

Judaism without tribalism: A system of Jewish teachings and traditions for the training of Jews in service to *teshuvah* and *tikkun*: respectively, returning to one's true nature as a manifesting of divine Aliveness (*chiut*), and repairing the world with justice and compassion in fulfillment of the Jew's mission to be a blessing to all the families of the earth (Genesis 12:3).

*

Jews are a tribe: an ancient and fractious family embracing multiple races, ethnicities, languages, customs, cuisines, ideas, and ideals. At the heart of our tribe is the story of Abram and Sarai, who felt called to leave their people, culture, and parents and to devote themselves to being a blessing to all the families of the earth (Genesis 12:1–3).

Being a blessing to person and planet is what being a Jew is all about. And because we are a tribe. we are always in danger of falling into tribalism: seeing our story as THE story and elevating our status above all other tribes on earth.

Judaism Without Tribalism is an attempt to articulate Judaism as a more open, welcoming, and universal path for Self-realization (teshuvah) and world repair (tikkun), in service to our original mission of being a blessing. In this way, we open the toolbox of Jewish practice to anyone and everyone.

While there is nothing wrong with being a tribe, tribalism is a dangerous perversion of Judaism. Tribalism mistakes story for history, parable for revelation, myth for science, and metaphor for fact. It shifts the focus of Judaism from being a means to an end—being a blessing to all the families of the earth—to being an end unto itself. Jews without tribalism argue over how best to be a blessing; Jews ensnared in tribalism argue over who is a Jew and what is authentic Judaism.

Judaism Without Tribalism is a brief book written in short sections set off by asterisks (*). I invite you to read this book slowly and consider its teachings carefully. This is a book to be pondered rather than digested. Its ideas are to be wrestled with rather than accepted.

My goal with this book, like my goal for all my Jewish

books, is to make Judaism accessible to everyone. I am not concerned with conversion or cultural appropriation. I am concerned with using the language and tools of Judaism to articulate what is universally true: *alles iz Gott*—everything is God.

WHAT IS JUDAISM WITHOUT TRIBALISM?

Judaism without tribalism is a Judaism rooted in, and devoted to, two foundational principles: teshuvah and tikkun—returning to your true nature as a manifesting of God and repairing the world with godliness.

Judaism without tribalism teaches that God is *YHVH* (from the Hebrew verb *h-y-h*, "to be"): the ineffable Happening happening as all happening. *YHVH* is not a noun but a verb, not a Being but being itself; not the Creator but creativity; not one separate from the many but a nondual and endless manifesting of the one and the many.

Judaism without tribalism teaches that all life is *tohu va-vohu*: intrinsically fluid, chaotic, absurd, and beyond your willful control (Genesis 1:2); and that each life is *hevel*: impermanent, empty of any eternal soul, and forever in the process of dying (Ecclesiastes 1:2). You can navigate the chaos, but you cannot manage it; you can push back against the absurdity, but you cannot defeat it; you can make meaning out of mortality, but you cannot escape it.

This is not, of course, the teaching of mainstream Judaism. Mainstream Judaism affirms a creator god who orders the universe, endows human beings with individual souls that survive bodily death, chooses the Jews, reveals the nature of things in Torah, and bestows upon his chosen the Land of Israel in perpetuity. The Judaism presented in this book is anything but mainstream.

The reason for this is simple: mainstream Judaism doesn't speak to me. My experience of life leads me to reject the notion of an ordered universe functioning according to divine will. My experience leads me to a realization of God beyond tribe, a realization that all reality is the happening of a nondual process called by many names: *YHVH*, Tao, Allah, Godhead, Mother, Brahman, Nature, etc. The Judaism that speaks to me—the Judaism I outline in this book—is rooted in those Jewish texts and teachings that point beyond tribalism toward truths that are not limited to any one tribe, people, or culture, and reflect instead reality as I perceive it.

Judaism without tribalism calls you to teshuvah: returning to your true nature as *tzelem elohim*: manifestings of the Divine, in the way that waves are manifestings of the ocean that waves them (Genesis 1:26).

Judaism without tribalism teaches that you are of two minds: *mochin d'katnut*, the narrow mind of self that is easily given over to *yetzer harah*, selfishness; and *mochin d'gadlut*, the spacious mind of Self that is easily given over to selflessness. The goal of Judaism is to place the former in service to the latter (Talmud, Berachot 61b).

Judaism without tribalism teaches that "it isn't good for people to be alone" (Genesis 2:18), and that our way is service to the wellbeing of person and planet (Leviticus 19:18, 32; Genesis 3:2).

Judaism without tribalism teaches that your mission in life is to be a caretaker of the natural world (Genesis 2:15) and to be a blessing to all the families of the earth (Genesis 12:3). You will fulfill this mission by doing justly, acting kindly, walking lightly (Micah 6:8), and not doing to others what you would consider hateful if it were done to you (Talmud, Shabbat 31a). In this way, you and others like you work toward a fearless world without war (Micah 4:3–4), where people eat simply, drink moderately, work joyously, and love freely (Ecclesiastes 2:24; 4:8–12). In this world, people seek Truth in their own way, bound together by shared questions rather than shared answers (Micah 4:5).

Judaism without tribalism does not teach that Jews are God's chosen people (Deuteronomy 14:2) to whom he gave his one and only revelation, plus a perpetual deed to the promised land. It does not teach that this god is obsessed with Jewish foreskins (Genesis 7:10–14; Leviticus 12:3); or is addicted to animal sacrifice (Exodus 20:21; Numbers 6:14; 28:15; 28:30; 29:5–6,11); or is jealous of every other god in the neighborhood (Exodus 5:9; 20:5; 34:14; Deuteronomy 4:24; 6:15; 32:16).

*

Judaism without tribalism calls for revolution, or it calls for nothing at all. Jews are either *ohr l'goyyim*, a light unto the nations (Isaiah 49:6), or we are irrelevant.

Our path is the iconoclasm of *lech lecha*: freeing ourselves from everything that keeps us from being a blessing to all the families of the earth, human and otherwise (Genesis 12:1–3).

Our pedagogy is *eilu v'eilu* (Eruvin 13b), honoring argument, doubt, and critical thinking over intellectual passivity, spiritual conformity, and manufactured consent.

Our tools are:

Shabbat, liberating all beings from *mitzrayim*, the narrow places of enslavement, and helping them reclaim their innate divinity (Deuteronomy 5:15; Exodus 20:8–10).

Kashrut, elevating manufacturing and consuming to the highest ethical and environmental standards.

Zedakah, the just use of money and capital.

Gemilut chasadim, the practice of lovingkindness.

Kavvanot, setting our intentions toward righteousness.

Shmirat halashon, cleansing our speech of gossip, slander, falsehood, and distortion.

Lishmoah, listening to the divine hum of Reality.

Limmud, turning Torah in search of wisdom.

Let us teach our children to invent the future and not preserve a frozen and romanticized past. If we are not about the future, we will find that we have none.

PART ONE
RELIGION

CHAPTER 1

RELIGION AT ITS BEST

Religion at its best honors the innate human drive to make meaning out of the chaos of Reality. Religion at its worst is the institutional effort to impose specific meaning on Reality.

Religion at its best is intrinsically creative, fluid, and evolving. Religion at its worst is intrinsically imitative, nostalgic, and resistant to change.

Religion at its best builds community based on common questions regarding the meaning and purpose of life. Religion at its worst imposes community based on enforced answers to these questions.

Religion at its best is at home with doubt. Religion at its worst is at home with dogmatic or unquestioning belief.

Religion at its best seeks to sharpen our questions. Religion at its worst seeks to silence our questioning.

Religion at its best sees belief as a stepping-stone to faith. Religion at its worst sees belief as a final "truth."

Religion at its best is a search for Truth. Religion at its worst is the acquiescence to shared beliefs.

Religion at its best is an act of inward searching. Religion at its worst is an act of outward conforming.

Religion at its best is inherently dangerous in that it leads toward the unknown. Religion at its worst is safe in that it leads toward already accepted behaviors and beliefs.

Religion at its best posits no beliefs. Religion at its worst insists upon them. Beliefs are affirmations of truth without any evidence that what is affirmed as truth is in fact true. For example, conventional Judaism believes that the Creator of the Universe chose the Jews from among all the peoples of the earth to receive his (sic) one and only revelation (Torah) and the deed to the Land of Israel. There is no evidence outside Jewish texts that this belief is true. And the insistence of Jewish texts that this is true is simply self-serving.

Every religion posits such self-serving beliefs, and it is because there is no proof that any of these beliefs is true that people of different religions hold different and often opposing beliefs. The fact that many Jews believe themselves to be chosen does not make them chosen, any more than the fact that many Christians believe Jesus is the Son of God makes Jesus the Son of God.

Think about this for a moment: Jews don't believe Jesus is the Son of God and reject as false the beliefs of those who do. This isn't an act of anti-Christian bias but a reflection of the fact that beliefs aren't truths but biases. Every religion confirms its own biases and rejects the biases of other religions.

Religion at its best recognizes this to be the case and sheds its biases/beliefs, leaving one naked before the existential facts of reality: that we are all expressions of a wild, glorious and chaotic process I call *YHVH*, a process capable of producing both light and dark, good and evil (Isaiah 45:7).

*

Religion at its best needs no defense. Religion at its worst needs armies.

Religion at its best welcomes testing, and those who

test truth are called sages. Religion at its worst eschews testing and calls those who test beliefs heretics.

Religion at its best honors the inner search for Truth. Religion at its worst outlaws that search and makes Truth a heresy.

In this book we will investigate Judaism as a religion at its best.

CHAPTER 2

RELIGION AND DEATH

Baruch Spinoza wrote, "The free person thinks least of all of death, and his wisdom is a meditation not on death but on life." With all due respect to Spinoza, whom I regard as one of the greatest Jewish thinkers of all time, I think he has this exactly backwards. Indeed, I would even go so far as to suggest that it is thinking about death that ultimately leads you to be free. I say this because my own meditations on death (and life, for that matter) have freed me from the illusion that I exist as a separate, temporarily embodied soul that existed prior to my birth and will continue to exist after my death.

Think about this: if you are a disembodied soul prior to birth and will remain such after bodily death, what is the point of being embodied in the first place? What does the disembodied soul not know that the embodied soul can come to learn? And if there is something the disembodied soul needs to learn, I cannot help but wonder why this is? Why would God create ignorant souls?

My understanding of life and death is best articulated in the metaphor of the ocean and wave. While each wave is unique and distinct, all waves are the happening of the ocean that waves them. No wave existed before the waving and no wave exists after the waving. The ocean in this analogy is *YHVH*, the Happening happening as all happening: God, if you like. The wave is you. Just as a wave is the temporary happening of the ocean, so you are a temporary happening of God. When you die you simply return to the source that waved you.

Contemplating death as your return to your true nature as a happening of *YHVH* is liberating; it frees you from having to cling to the temporary "you" and allows you to take refuge in the eternal divine.

With this in mind, let's dive into the relation of religion and death.

*

You are going to die. Maybe today. Certainly tomorrow.

There are two basic responses to this fact: 1) Holy shit! I'm going to die! and 2) Holy shit! I'm still alive!

If you respond with the former, your energy is captured by death and how best to avoid it. If you respond with the latter, your energy is captured by life and how best to live it.

Conventional religions avoid death by positing a personal afterlife. I'm not talking about the death of your body—almost every religion accepts that though some get around that by positing a return to your body in some future time. I'm talking about the death of your "self," your personality, the "you" that you associate with your body regardless of the changes your body undergoes. If you believe that this "you" survives bodily death, if you believe you will have a life in some afterlife, if you believe in an eternal soul separate from all other souls that is uniquely you, you are avoiding death.

Of course, I am aware that many, if not most, people do affirm such a soul. I simply ascribe this belief to the ego's need to imagine itself immortal. Sticking with my ocean/wave analogy, no wave outlasts its waving. This may be depressing to some, but not to me. To me it is liberating.

My true nature is the ocean, God, and my embodied self is simply an expression of God in time and space. Death simply returns me to what I already am.

If, as I argue, avoiding death is the promise of conventional religion, then Judaism without tribalism focuses on living wisely with dying. If religion imagines that there is a way out of death, then Judaism without tribalism helps you to make meaning out of the life you have.

Different religions deny death through various beliefs: heaven and hell, reincarnation, rebirth in other worlds or in other dimensions—but they all hold out the promise that you will not die a permanent death. Because we don't wish to die a permanent death, we imagine religions that promise us a way to escape death.

The problem is this: with so many religions to choose from, and almost all of them offering a Get Out of Death Free Card, how do you know which religion is the right religion? Which religion's Get Out of Death Free Card actually leads to immortality? Pick the wrong one and you die. Or worse: pick the wrong one and you don't die but spend eternity burning in Hell. The challenge is to discern which religion is right about how to escape death.

Sadly, there is no way to determine which religion is right. This is because all religions are based on beliefs: affirmations of truth that cannot be verified or falsified. Let me expand on this a moment.

I live in a community dominated by evangelical Christians, almost all of whom believe I am going to Hell because I do not accept Jesus as my Lord and Savior. They are certain they are right about this. And because their belief—like all belief—can neither be proven nor disproven, they may be right. Should I accept Jesus as my Lord and Savior just to be safe?

When I put this option to rabbi friends of mine, they affirm that acceptance of Jesus is not the criterion necessary for access to Heaven. How do they know? Their Jewish belief tells them so. But how do I know they are right?

I could complicate matters even further and ask for the beliefs of my friends who are imams and swamis. But adding opinions doesn't solve my problem. Every religion asserts it is correct, but none can prove their assertion nor disprove the assertion of the others. Worrying about this will simply drive you crazy.

There is a way out of this madness: realize religions are competing clubs with their own self-serving beliefs and opt out of the game of trying to determine which one is true. This doesn't mean you have to stop being a Jew, a Christian, a Moslem, a Hindu, or anything else. It only means that you stop imagining that your chosen club is true.

*

Judaism has no fixed notion of an afterlife: you can believe what you want about what happens after you die, including that nothing happens. Judaism simply isn't concerned with the afterlife. That is why our motto is *l'Chayyim*: "To life!"

As the sage and heretic Baruch Spinoza wrote, "Free people think of death least of all. Their wisdom is a meditation not on death but on life" (Ethics Part 4).

The question Judaism asks isn't "How will you spend eternity after you die?", but "How will you spend the years you have before you die?" That is the better question.

Here is the question that will occupy us throughout this book: How shall we live the one life we have in a manner that fulfills our mission to be a blessing to all the families of the earth? (Genesis 12:3).

CHAPTER 3

GOD AND GODS

What is true of gods is not true of God. As the creation of their tribe, a god is tasked with buttressing the power of tribal leaders and endorsing the policies these leaders seek to impose on other human beings. God is something else.

Some people want a personal god for the same reason they want a personal lover: for the intimacy and the security.

The problem with a personal god is the same as with a personal lover: you can never take that intimacy and security for granted. So, you are forever anxious. To earn your beloved's love, you agree to do whatever it is you imagine your beloved wants.

When it comes to a personal god, however, all you know is what your god's professional spokespeople want you to know. These spokespeople are called theologians. Theologians are rarely free agents, and most theologians work for a specific god within a specific religion.

Because each theologian works for one particular god, their ideas about God are always in service to that god. This is why Jewish theologians never discover that the Hopi are god's chosen people rather than the Jews, and why Christian theologians never discover that the Holy Trinity is Brahma, Vishnu, and Shiva rather than Father, Son, and Holy Spirit.

Theologians only "discover" what they already believe to be true. This is confirmation bias masquerading as revelation. This is useful if you are promoting a specific god but useless if you are seeking God beyond the gods of conventional religion. Of course, there are theologians who transcend religion. For example, Martin Buber's *Eternal Thou Isn't Jewish* and Paul Tillich's *Ground of All Being Isn't Christian*. But these are exceptions to the rule. Go to any library or bookstore and you'll find that the vast majority of books written by authors of one religion or another are promoting the god of their own religion.

People routinely create gods in their own image for the purpose of securing their own status, power, and authority. Thus, the gods they create always prefer their creators, and the descendants of their creators, to other people. The status of a religion is proportionate to the power of its god to dominate other gods and their followers. The power of that god is directly related to the power of its army. This is why Judaism is a minor religion everywhere but in the State of Israel where the Jewish god and his army reign supreme.

*

God, as I use the word, refers not to any tribal deity, or to any named god, but to the greater Reality manifesting in, with, and as all being.

God is not a noun, but a verb. As a verb, God cannot be owned by any tribe or authority. But as a noun, god is always owned.

God as a verb is revealed to us through the parable of Moses and the burning bush (Exodus 3:1–15). In this story, Moses is shepherding his father-in-law's flocks, as he has done for decades. This time, however, he notices a bush on fire that is not consumed by the fire. Curious,

Moses draws close to the burning bush and encounters God. Not the Israelite god, but God—the unnamed and fundamentally unnamable God.

God tells Moses to remove his sandals because he is standing on sacred ground (Exodus 3:5). Sandals keep our feet from coming into direct contact with the ground. So, in effect, God says to Moses, Remove everything that keeps you from coming into direct contact with the Ground of all Being.

In our own lives, this means removing any names we have for god; freeing ourselves from our tribal gods; and standing godless before God. This is something each of us must do if we are to realize Truth.

*

In tribalist Judaism, god is Adonai, lord. But in Judaism without tribalism, God is *YHVH*, a variation of the Hebrew verb "to be."

The verb *YHVH* lacks all vowels and is therefore literally unpronounceable. This is not an accident. *YHVH* is the Tao that cannot be named (*Tao Te Ching*: 1). If you cannot pronounce the name of God, you cannot reduce God to god, since all gods have pronounceable names. If you cannot reduce *YHVH* to a god, *YHVH* always points beyond the tribal to the universal. *YHVH* is the God of all Reality; indeed, *YHVH* is Reality itself.

An unnamable God is a God beyond the control of tribal leaders.

Because *YHVH* is beyond control, the early rabbis had to invent a god that was controllable. Since they inherited the name *YHVH* from the Hebrew Bible, they couldn't simply abandon it. But, since the name *YHVH* was literally unpronounceable, they could create a euphemism that would in time replace *YHVH* in the minds of the

Jewish people, and that could be placed in service of the rabbis. That euphemism was Adonai, "Lord." Wherever the verb *YHVH* appears in the Bible, the rabbis have ruled that the reader is to say Adonai instead.

The god Adonai is male, hierarchical, and all about power and control. This suited the rabbis of emerging Judaism, who were also male, hierarchical, and all about power and control.

When the rabbis translated the Hebrew Bible into Greek (the Septuagint) in the third century BCE, they effectively wrote *YHVH* out of the Bible by replacing the Hebrew verb *YHVH* with the Greek noun Kyrios, which also means Lord. Later translations influenced by the Septuagint continued the practice, which is why English Bibles never speak of *YHVH*, but only of Lord.

*

After removing his sandals, Moses experiences God commanding him to return to Egypt—*Mitzrayim* in Hebrew—and liberate the enslaved (Exodus 3:10). Mitzrayim is a Hebrew play on words meaning "the narrow places." The unnamed and unnamable *YHVH*, the God beyond tribe and tribalism, is concerned with only one thing: human liberation.

Knowing that people cannot easily grasp a God they cannot name, Moses asks God for a name. God, to avoid the tribalism that comes with a brand-name god, replies with two: *Ehyeh asher Ehyeh* (Exodus 3:14) and *YHVH* (Exodus 3:15). Neither name is a proper noun. Both names are verbs, variations of the Hebrew verb "to be." *Ehyeh asher Ehyeh* is Being, experienced from the "inside"; *YHVH* is Being experienced from the "outside."

Ehyeh asher Ehyeh, often translated as "I am becoming what I am becoming," is pure happening seen from the inside by the singular I, Ehyeh. *YHVH* is the same happening, seen from the outside. *YHVH* is the term we use when pointing to God happening around us. Ehyeh is the term we use when we awaken to the reality that God is us.

Imagine all existence to be the waving of an ocean. Each wave is unique and distinct, yet no wave is apart from the ocean that waves it. From the ocean's point of view, all waves are an extension of itself. If the ocean could speak, it would say, "I am waving." This is the ocean as Ehyeh.

But from a wave's point of view, each wave is something the ocean is doing. If the wave could speak, it would say, "The ocean is waving me." This is the ocean as *YHVH*.

*

A major difference between god and God is that a god requires belief, while God requires knowing.

Belief is an affirmation of something we do not know to be true but nevertheless insist must be true. It must be true because if it isn't true, the entire edifice on which god rests crumbles.

Knowing has nothing to do with belief. Knowing is rooted instead in experience.

While you may choose to believe in one god or another, you don't choose to believe in God. Instead you experience God in, with, and as all things. You experience God as the very aliveness (*chiut* in Hebrew) of all Reality. You don't believe in chiut; you experience chiut in this and every moment.

No one can prove that god chose the Jews from among all the peoples of the earth. No one can prove that god didn't, either. All we can do is choose to believe or not believe this tribal claim.

Beliefs can be crazy-making. I can't prove or disprove that god chose the Jews, or that god incarnated as Jesus, or that god incarnated as Krishna, or that god dictated the Holy Qur'an to Mohammad. Not only can I not prove or disprove any of these things, but I can't even test them. That is the problem with belief: it is unverifiable.

Judaism without tribalism deals with experience, not belief.

Judaism without tribalism means a Judaism without god. But not a Judaism without God.

When I speak of *YHVH*, I'm speaking of God as the Happening happening as all happening. I'm speaking of God as chiut, the divine Aliveness happening as every life. I am not speaking of Adonai, Lord, the tribal god of the Jews.

*

YHVH "creates" the universe the way an ocean "creates" waves. Just as waves are the ocean, so creation is *YHVH*. Just as there can be no wave separate from the ocean, so there is nothing other than God.

This is what Judaism means by the phrase *ein od milvado*, "there is no other" (Deuteronomy 4:35). Understood through the distorting lens of tribal craziness, ein od milvado means "There is no god other than the Jewish god." But understood directly, without that lens, ein od milvado means "There is nothing other than God."

This understanding is not unique to me. Listen to the following four Jewish sages whose experience of *YHVH* as chiut, divine Aliveness, led them to the same understanding of God:

The Spanish Kabbalist Moshe Cordovero (1522–1570) wrote, "God is found in all things and all things are found in God.... Everything is in God, and God is in everything and beyond everything, and there is nothing beside God, ein od milvado."

Schneur Zalman of Liadi (1745–1813), the founder of Chabad Hasidism, wrote, "Everything is God who makes everything be, and in truth the world of seemingly separate entities is entirely annulled."

Reb Noson (1780–1844), the chief disciple of Reb Nachman of Breslov (1772–1810), wrote, "Ein od milvado means nothing exists other than *YHVH*. Above and below, in heaven and on earth, every seemingly separate thing is absolutely empty and without substance—although this is impossible to explain and can only be grasped according to the intuition of each person."

Menachem Mendel Schneerson (1902–1994), the last rebbe of Chabad Hasidism, wrote, "The absolute reality of God, while extending beyond the conceptual borders of existence, also fills the entire expanse of existence as we know it. There is no space possible for any other existences or realities we may identify—the objects of our physical universe, the metaphysical truths we contemplate, our very selves ... do not exist in their own reality; they exist only as an extension of divine energy."

*

Most people imagine the Jewish god as a supreme being who is separate from creation. But there are rabbis who see beyond this god to God—beyond god as the creator to God as creation, beyond god as other to God as all.

As we say in Yiddish, *Alles iz Gott*: everything is God.

Because everything is God, nature is God. This is what Baruch Spinoza (1632–1677) taught when he spoke of *Deus sive Natura*, "God or Nature." Nature is a manifesting of God, but God is greater still. Again, think of an ocean and its waves. While the ocean is all of its waves, the sum of its waves are not all of the ocean. The ocean is greater still. God, *YHVH*, is always "greater still."

*

Because God is nature and nature evolves—God, too, evolves. The direction of God's evolution, the direction of chiut—aliveness—is toward higher levels of consciousness and broader circles of compassion.

The more you release the god of tribalism, the more aware you become of God as aliveness, and the more sacred life becomes. The more sacred life becomes, the more compassionate you are toward the living—and the more you engage with life justly, kindly, and humbly (Micah 6:8).

Tribal gods also change. That's why the god of Torah is so often angry and violent, while the god of the ancient rabbis and their Gospel-writing contemporaries is often compassionate and kind. The angry god was created in the image of a powerful priesthood who, in consort with Jewish kings and Roman emperors, sought to impose their will on people through force. The compassionate god was a god created in the image of powerless sages and wandering evangelists, who operated without political sanction or military backing.

Sadly, the compassionate god changed back into the militaristic god when the Church became the Holy Roman Empire, and the rabbis became the theocrats of the modern State of Israel. Beware of gods with armies.

*

A major attraction of any god is the notion that god loves you. The love of god, however, is contingent on you obeying god—or, rather, obeying the laws of those who claim to speak in the name of god. For example: "If you conscientiously obey my commandments and love me and serve me, then I will send the seasonal rains to irrigate your fields that they may yield much grain, grapes, and olives. And I will provide your cattle with grass that they grow fat and you will eat and be satisfied. But, if you turn away from me and worship other gods, then my anger will rage against you, and I will close the sky and cut off the rain so that the earth is barren, and you will quickly die" (Deuteronomy 11:13–17).

People turn to god for security and protection from the harshness of life. But security and protection are not gifts that God provides. God cannot protect you from the horrors of life because God includes the horrors of life. Just as an ocean may be calm in one area and roiling in another, so God may be life-giving in one moment and life-taking in another. *YHVH* is the Happening happening as all happening—happenings we like and happenings we don't like: "I manifest light and darkness. I create good and evil. I, *YHVH*, do all things" (Isaiah 45:7).

Knowing that *YHVH* includes all opposites, you cannot seek to embrace good and avoid evil. You cannot escape the dark and take refuge in the light. Good and evil, dark and light, go together as *up* goes with *down* and *in* goes with *out*. This is what Job tells us when he urges us to "accept the good as well as the bad from God" (Job 2:10).

Knowing that good and evil are both part of God frees you from the craziness of religious authorities who promise a god who will protect you from evil and harm. It also frees you from the double craziness in which religious authorities and their god fail to protect you from evil and harm—and then those authorities turn around and blame you for not believing strongly enough. They insist that, through your tepid belief, you brought the evil and harm upon yourself. It isn't their god who has failed you, they say, but you who failed god.

*

One of the simplest ways to distinguish between god and God is that god always needs money, while God never does.

Another way to distinguish between god and God is that god always has clergy, and often has armies. This god is always on the lookout for people who worship in the wrong way—i.e., outside the control of the clergy.

Torah warns us of this in the story of Aaron's sons Nadab and Abihu. Out of a great love for god, the two brothers made an unauthorized offering to god. Rather than rewarding the boys for their devotion, however, god engulfs them in flames, and they die horribly (Leviticus 10:1–2).

What can we make of this story? Making an unauthorized offering challenges the power of the clergy, who determine what is authorized and what is not authorized, what god wants and when god wants it. If you can worship god as you please and when you please, the clergy have no power over you. That is something neither they nor their god can abide.

*

People often say that god is unknowable, but this is clearly not the case. If god were unknowable, there would be no religion. After all, the entire conceit of religion is that it knows what god wants and needs in order to gift you with what you want and need. If god is unknowable, there is no point in praying to god. Indeed, if god is unknowable, there may be no god to whom you can pray.

All gods are knowable, and religion is the way you know them.

Religions may claim that god is unknowable, but they do so only to avoid having to explain why god does such horrible things to those who love god.

YHVH is always knowable. *YHVH* is chiut, aliveness, the Happening happening as all happening. You know *YHVH* through science. You know *YHVH* through contemplative practice. You know *YHVH* when you know yourself. As Job said, "In my flesh I see God!" (Job 19:26).

You also know *YHVH* when you know "the design of the universe, the forces of nature, the nature of time, the orbits of suns and stars, the changing of the seasons, the cycles of years, the minds of animals both domesticated and wild, the power of the wind, the workings of the human mind, the medicinal powers of plants and roots" (Wisdom of Solomon 7:17–22).

Yet we cannot know all of *YHVH*. Reality is always subtler than our most subtle insights, and grander than our most grand theories, and weirder than even the weirdest of our quantum imaginings. There is always room for surprise.

But never room for control. Religion promises us the capacity to control god. Judaism without tribalism expands our capacity to live meaningfully without control.

*

People often say, "We all worship the same god." This is nonsense. And those who say it are simply trying to avoid the fact that we all worship different gods; that the gods we worship are often antithetical to one another; and that their antipathy can lead us to acts of terror in the name of our god.

Muslims and Jews worship a god who has no son, while

Christians worship a god who does. To a Christian, if god has no son, then god isn't god at all. The Jewish god wrote Torah and had nothing to do with the Holy Qur'an, the Gospels, or the Bhagavad Gita. Lord Ganesha, who did write the Bhagavad Gita, had nothing to do with Torah, the Gospels, and the Holy Qur'an. Not a single one of the gods worshipped by Hindus dabbles in real estate, yet the Jewish god gave the Jews the deed to the Land of Israel in perpetuity.

The gods we worship are the invention of those who profit from them. These gods reflect the desires, biases, hopes, and dreams of their inventors. To insist that we all worship the same god is to deny the uniqueness of each god and the people who worship that god.

Having different gods is not in and of itself a problem. The problem arises from what one god tells you to do about all the other gods. When your god tells you to assassinate peacemakers like Gandhi and Yitzchak Rabin; when your god tells you to fly planes into buildings; when your god tells you to oppress or murder Palestinians, Jews, Blacks, Hispanics, Asians, queer folk, Muslims, Christians, Hindus, or Buddhists; when your god tells you to believe that people who don't believe as you believe are destined to spend eternity burning in hell, you can be certain that your god isn't God.

*

God is *YHVH*, the Happening happening as all happening. *YHVH* is chiut, aliveness. Anything people do that diminishes life and the lives of others is taking God's name in vain.

Given that it is so easy for us to use god to sanction evil, it is crazy to imagine that one cannot be good without god—or that, with god on your side, you always do good. In fact, you might be a better person without god, since as Blaise Pascal (1623–1662) wrote, "People never do evil so completely and cheerfully as when they do it from religious conviction."

God and god differ when it comes to evil, but neither God nor god puts an end to it. Evil is a category of behavior limited to human beings. A pandemic—even one that takes the lives of millions of people—isn't evil. It's simply part of nature, and hence a happening of God as *YHVH*.

Evil is what people do to one another. Evil isn't when you are stricken with a terrible illness; evil is when your health insurance company employs an army of lawyers to avoid having to cover your medical treatment.

God doesn't prevent evil because evil is a part of God, who is all Reality. Tribal gods don't prevent evil because they are figments of a tribe's imagination.

The question to ask regarding evil isn't: Why does God (or god) allow evil? The questions to ask are: Why do I do evil, and how do I respond to the evil done by others, especially when it is done in the name of god?

The best way to respond to evil done in the name of your god is, first, to "turn from evil and do good" (Psalm 34:14), and then to turn away from your god altogether. A god without followers is powerless.

Sadly, most people who believe in a god cannot turn away from that god so easily. Instead, they seek to excuse their god from evil.

*

Free will is how most people excuse their god from being responsible for evil. People say they need free will so they can choose for themselves how to behave. The truth is that people need free will so they can punish other people for how they choose to behave—and so they can avoid blaming god for how these other people behave.

People insist on free will because it exonerates god from the evil people do: "Evil isn't god's fault; it's something we humans choose; god had to give us free will because, without free will, we couldn't love god freely. Instead, we would be programmed to love god against our will." Of course, if we were all programmed by god to love god, then no one would go to hell for disbelieving in god.

Instead, we are told, we have heaven and hell, and the ability to choose one or the other. The invention of these realms makes folks who believe in god feel special and superior.

This is what Thomas Aquinas (1225–1274) admits in his *Summa Theolgica*: "No joy shall be denied those who are welcomed into heaven, and in order to increase their joy and to make their experience in heaven all the more delightful to them, they are allowed to peer into hell and see without distortion the sufferings of the damned."

As much as we like to imagine that we have free will, we also like to imagine that god has free will as well. If god lacks free will, then god can't change his/her/their mind in response to our prayers.

Yet *YHVH* does lack free will. *YHVH* cannot be other than *YHVH*. Since *YHVH* is the Happening happening as all happening, God is all that is. And since God is all that is, God cannot be other than what is. God isn't free to be other than God, and no amount of piety, prayer, or generosity can change that.

*

Sin is not complicated. Since the core mission of humankind is to care for creation (Genesis 2:15) and be a blessing to all the families of the earth (Genesis 12:3), sin is any action that works against the thriving of people or the planet.

In Judaism without tribalism, our response to sin is simple: "turn from evil and do good; seek peace and pursue peace" (Psalm 34:14); act in service of people and Planet Earth.

*

People like to believe that god has a plan for their lives. The plan god has for them is always good, because the god that plans it is always good. If something bad happens to you, it is part of a greater plan that is ultimately good.

Because god's plan for your life is always good, believing that god has a plan for your life is always comforting.

Of course, the plan that god has for your life always coincides with the religion you follow. For example, god's plan for a Jew is to be a more observant Jew, not to become a Catholic. Or god's plan for a Muslim is to be a better Muslim, not to become a Hindu, even a very good one.

Maybe *YHVH* doesn't have a plan for your life. *YHVH* is the Happening happening as all happening. Things only happen when the conditions for their happening are present to such a degree that nothing else can happen. That's why it never rains in the Dry Valleys of Antarctica. The weather conditions in the Dry Valleys are such that the Dry Valleys haven't seen rainfall in two million years.

Living a long and fruitful life isn't a reward from god but the result of circumstances that make living a long and fruitful life inevitable. The same is true if you live a long and fruitless life, or a short and fruitful one, or even a short and fruitless one.

Maybe there is no plan, only Reality.

PART TWO
JEWS

CHAPTER 4

WHO IS A JEW?

A Jew is a person who claims to be a Jew.

This is not the official definition of who is a Jew—indeed, there is no one official definition, only definitions held by different groups of Jews—but it is the only definition that is free of tribalism and crazymaking.

Some Jews object to the idea that a Jew is anyone who calls themselves a Jew because it allows anyone to be a Jew. That's true. But so what? What is the downside if one hundred million people who did not call themselves Jews yesterday decide to do so tomorrow? Is this going to dilute the Jewish gene pool? No. There is no Jewish gene pool. If there were, then only people with Jewish blood could be Jews. But, since we can't agree as to who is a Jew, we can't agree as to whose blood is Jewish either.

The reason we can't agree on who is a Jew is because we can't agree on a body of officials empowered to define who is a Jew. One of the oddest things about Jews is our inability to define who is a Jew. On the other hand, not agreeing on things having to doing with Judaism turns out to be a hallmark of being a Jew.

*

Old joke: a Jew is rescued after years of being stranded alone on a desert island. He takes his rescuers on a tour to show them how he has survived all these years. Among his accomplishments is the building of two synagogues.

Astonished, his rescuers ask him why he built two synagogues instead of just one.

The man points to one of the two and says, "This is the synagogue I always attend." He then points to the other and says, "This is the synagogue I would never set foot in."

*

Most Jews are Jews by default. That is to say, someone told them they were Jews, so they tell themselves and others that they are Jews. The central practice of Jews by default is paying attention to the news and hoping that Jews are not among the victims—or the perpetrators—of the day's negative headlines.

*

Some Jews argue that a Jew is a person who cares about the question "Who is a Jew?" The problem with this answer is that antisemites—or, more accurately, Jew-haters—are no less obsessed with the question. While Jews want to know who a Jew is so they can count them in the tribal tally, Jew-haters want to know who a Jew is so they can count them out of the human tally.

*

Most Jews argue that a Jew is a person who is born to a Jewish mother (or, according to some, a Jewish father). I am not one of them.

I once received an e-mail from a woman who, as an infant, had been adopted by a Catholic family. She was raised as a Catholic and, as an adult, became a nun. She recently discovered that her biological mother was Jewish. "Does this mean I'm a Jew?" she asked me. According to some Jews, this Catholic nun is a Jew. This is crazy.

If your mother is a ballerina, does that make you a ballerina? Having a ballerina for a mother might make you curious about ballet; it might incline you to take ballet lessons; it might even lead you to devote your life to ballet. But you might also have no interest in ballet at all. Similarly, having a Jewish mother (or father) may make you curious about Judaism; it might incline you to study Hebrew and Torah and to experiment with Jewish tradition. It might even lead you to devote your life to Judaism. But anyone can do that, whether they have a Jewish mother (or father) or not.

*

Most humans don't want to be Jews. Even some Jews don't want to be Jews. If you don't want to be a Jew, don't be one, and stop calling yourself a Jew. Even if you are part of the seventh generation of a long Haredi ("ultraorthodox") lineage, if you don't want to be a Jew and don't call yourself a Jew, for all practical purposes you are not a Jew in anyone's eyes. Except in the eyes of Jew-haters, who will see you as a Jew even if you become a Catholic nun.

*

Some people who do call themselves Jews don't want to learn anything about Jewish history, Jewish holy days, Jewish texts and literature, and Jewish traditions. They just like calling themselves Jews and have no interest in teshuvah or tikkun or being a blessing. So why call yourself a Jew? Outside of the State of Israel, where Jewish tribalism privileges the Jew, there is no advantage to calling yourself a Jew. So, in my opinion, if you want nothing to do with Judaism, stop calling yourself a Jew.

*

Some people think Jews are a race. This is nonsense. Since all humans are 99.9 percent genetically identical with one another, there is only one race: the human race. Jews are part of that race.

Some who think of Jews as a race think of Jews as a white race. This isn't only false—Jews come in all of humanity's hues—it is racist.

*

Some people who agree that Jews are not a race insist that Jews are a distinct ethnic group. This too is false. Jews embrace multiple ethnicities. There are Iranian Jews, Iraqi Jews, Egyptian Jews, Sudanese Jews, Tunisian Jews, Algerian Jews, Moroccan Jews, Lebanese Jews, Kurdish Jews, Libyan Jews, Syrian Jews, Indian Jews, Ethiopian Jews, Bukharan Jews, Chinese Jews, Ashkenazi (Germanic) Jews, Sephardic (Spanish) Jews, Lemba (South African) Jews—the list goes on. Each of these ethnicities has its own cuisine, music, customs, understanding of Judaism, and language. What makes all these people Jews is that they all say they are Jews.

*

Jews are a tribe, an extended three-thousand-plus-year-old family.

In ancient times, there were twelve tribes of Israel (Deuteronomy 33:6–25). Each tribe traced its origins back to one of the twelve sons of Jacob and one or another of his two wives, Leah and Rachel, and his two concubines, Zilpah and Bilhah.

In 930 BCE, ten of the tribes established the Northern Kingdom of Israel. The tribe of Judah established the Southern Kingdom of Judah. The tribe of Benjamin split itself between them.

When the Assyrians conquered the Northern Kingdom in 721 BCE, the ten tribes disappeared as distinct tribal bodies. The remaining Benjaminites were assimilated into the tribe of Judah.

In 586 BCE, the Babylonians destroyed Judah. In 538 BCE, Cyrus the Great, ruler of the Achaemenian Empire, allowed the people of Judah to return from their exile in Babylonia to what was now a Persian province called Yahud.

Seven hundred years later, when the Romans put down a revolt by the messianic rebel Bar Kochba, Roman legions decimated that land, which they called Judea, and exiled most (but not all) Judeans.

*

As with most families, we Jews argue among ourselves incessantly. As with most families, there are members of our family we would like to forget. Also as with most families, we can't agree on which members of the family we would like to forget.

And, as with most families, there are members of the family who believe one thing about being a member of the family, and members of the family who believe the opposite. Nevertheless, as with most families, no matter what our various members say or do or think, we are still family.

*

One hallmark of our family is hospitality. In biblical times, it was customary to close the flaps of one's tent as a defense against the intrusion of strangers. But Jewish tradition tells us that Abraham and Sarah, the first Jews, lifted the flaps of their tent as a sign of welcome, offering hospitality to all who might pass by: "When they saw travelers coming toward them, they would run out to greet them" (Midrash Rabbah 48:9).

Hospitality toward strangers is enshrined in Torah: "You shall show respect to the stranger for you know what it is to be a stranger" (Deuteronomy 10:19).

For centuries, Jews welcomed "the stranger" and adopted into the extended Jewish family anyone who wished to associate themselves with Jews and Judaism: "Your people shall be my people; your god shall be my god," as Ruth said to her mother-in-law Naomi (Ruth 1:16).

All of this ended in the fourth century CE, when the Holy Roman Empire forbade such hospitality—and executed rabbis who engaged in it. The Church's foreclosure on Jewish hospitality to gentiles led to widespread distrust of gentiles among many Jews—a distrust that continues to play itself out today. Nevertheless, Jews who follow a Judaism without tribalism continue to leave our tent flaps open to all who are curious about who we are and what we do and teach.

*

Many years ago, when my father and I were touring Israel, we spent Shabbat at a hotel in Haifa. During dinner, my dad was intrigued by a large party of Iraqi Jews. Never having encountered brown-skinned Jews before, he insisted on going over to their table and speaking to them, in the hopes of learning more. I tried to dissuade him because, while many Iraqi Jews speak Hebrew, my dad didn't—and, while my dad spoke fluent Yiddish, chances were that these Iraqi Jews didn't.

My father ignored my logic, walked over to their table, and introduced himself in English. He soon learned that the dinner party was part of a family reunion. One family member was a professor from Cincinnati, Ohio, who, of course, spoke English. The family welcomed my dad into their midst, and he spent the entire Sabbath with them. I spent Shabbat at the Baha'i Shrine of the Bab on Mount Carmel. Family.

*

Given the dysfunction and argumentation that marks the Jewish family, it shouldn't surprise anyone that we divide ourselves into smaller divisions called denominations. The major denominations are Orthodox, Conservative, Reconstructionist, Renewal, Reform, and Humanist. Simply put, though many would argue with me over this, denominations differ from one another primarily over their relationship to rabbinic law and tradition.

Orthodox and Conservative Judaisms seek to approx-imate themselves to the past, while still accommodating Judaism to the present. They differ as to which accommo-dations are allowed and which are not. While Conservative Jews allow for more flexibility than Orthodox Jews, both denominations see the changes they make as necessary to maintaining fealty to the past. The role of Orthodox and Conservative rabbis is to determine which changes are allowed and which are not.

Reconstructionist and Renewal Judaisms look at the past as a resource for Jewish creativity in the present. The role of the rabbi in these Judaisms is to educate the com-munity in the resources available to them and to guide their respective communities in adapting these resources to the needs of the community, in order to enrich the life of the community. As my teacher Rabbi Mordecai Kaplan, the founder of Reconstructionist Judaism, taught: "The past has a vote, but not a veto" when it comes to determining what is authentic Judaism in the present.

While Orthodox, Conservative, Reconstructionist, and Renewal Judaisms are rooted in the centrality of community, Reform Judaism, especially in its early and most radical days, placed the individual rather than the community at the center of Judaism. The individual Jews, rather than the Jewish community or its rabbis, are to decide for themselves what is Jewish. The Reform rabbi's role is to teach and empower each individual to observe tradition as they see fit: "We accept as binding only the moral laws and maintain only such ceremonies as elevate and sanctify our lives" (Pittsburgh Platform 1885). It is up to the individual to determine just what it means to sanctify their life.

Humanistic Judaism is similar to Reform Judaism in that it empowers the individual to be the arbiter of their Judaism but differs from Reform and all other denominations in that it openly rejects the existence of a supernatural god and all hope in divine intervention. I say "openly" because, as most surveys of Jews will tell you, most Jews reject supernaturalism; they just keep that rejection to themselves and make no effort to recast Judaism in a secular or humanistic frame. The role of the Humanistic rabbis is to foster a sense of Jewish identity without reliance on theology or tradition.

*

In the interest of full disclosure: I was born into Orthodox Judaism and raised as an Orthodox Jew until I was fourteen, when my Orthodox synagogue aligned itself with Conservative Judaism, and my mom could sit with my dad during worship services.

After graduate school, where I wrote my thesis on Rabbi Kaplan and Reconstructionist Judaism, I attended Hebrew Union College-Jewish Institute of Religion and was ordained as a Reform Rabbi. While studying at HUC-JIR, I was mentored by Rabbi Sherwin Wine, the founder of Humanistic Judaism, and spent two years as editor of Humanistic Judaism magazine.

Upon graduation, I became the rabbi of an unaffiliated synagogue, which I led into the Reconstructionist Movement. A few years later I met and became a disciple of Reb Zalman Schachter-Shalomi, the founder of the neo-Hasidic Jewish Renewal Movement. I received private ordination from Reb Zalman decades later.

My point: I find wisdom in all forms of Judaism but feel called to restrict myself to none.

*

Thousands of people convert to Judaism each year. Given that Jews can't agree on who is a Jew or how to be a Jew, conversion to Judaism is problematic. A person who converts through a more liberal form of Judaism may not be accepted as a Jew by a more orthodox form of Judaism. But the greater problem is with the idea of conversion itself.

Conversion requires one to replace one set of beliefs with another. For example, a Christian who converts to Judaism is expected to jettison her belief in Jesus as the messiah in favor of the Jewish notion that the messiah, if there even is one, has not yet come.

Beliefs are cherished ideas for which there is no evidence. Given that there is no evidence proving the veracity of any religious belief, you might imagine changing beliefs would be easy. You would be mistaken. Beliefs don't rest on reason, but on emotion, and emotional attachments are often very hard to discard. And, if all religious beliefs are affirmations of sacred opinion rather than actual truths, why substitute one set of beliefs for another? This is like replacing belief in Santa Claus with belief in the Tooth Fairy.

Because this is so, I replace conversion to Judaism with adoption of Judaism.

*

The most common way people are adopted into the Jewish family is through marriage. Just as marrying someone makes you a part of your partner's family, marrying a Jew makes you part of the Jewish family. This is often called intermarriage.

Many Jews fear intermarriage between Jews and people who are not Jews. They are afraid that if you aren't born into a Jewish family and raised as a Jew, you will not choose to be a Jew. Underlying this fear is the unspoken notion that no one in their right mind would choose to be a Jew.

One way to deal with intermarriage is to stop calling it intermarriage. It's just marriage, and as with most marriages, each partner marries into the family of the other. Over time, elements of both families will find a place in the life of the married couple.

If your Judaism is tribalist, however, you will find this notion troubling. You want the couple to be exclusively Jewish. But if your Judaism is not tribalist—if it is based on the principles of teshuvah (returning to your true nature as a manifesting of God/*YHVH*), and tikkun (repairing the world with justice and compassion), in service to being a blessing to all the families of the earth, you are not concerned with exclusivity. You are just happy to have another family member taking up the task of being a blessing.

CHAPTER 5

GOD-WRESTLERS

Asking, "Who is a Jew?", as we did in the previous chapter, raises the issue of identity. Asking, "What is a Jew?", as we are in this chapter, asks about the essence or the core quality of being a Jew. For me, that core quality is being a god-wrestler.

Before Jews were called Jews, we were called Yisrael. The name means "one who wrestles with (*yisra*) god (*el*)." This comes from the story about our ancestor Jacob.

Traveling home with his wives, children, servants, flocks, and possessions, Jacob learns that his brother Esau is approaching with four hundred soldiers. Knowing that his brother has sworn to kill him for stealing their father's deathbed blessing, which rightly belonged to Esau (Genesis 27), Jacob takes his party across Jabbok's Ford, and then returns to face his brother alone. As he waits, he is attacked by an angel.

The two wrestle throughout the night. When the angel sees that he cannot defeat Jacob, he wounds Jacob in the hip, leaving him permanently impaired. Still, Jacob does not let the angel go.

As dawn approaches, the angel calls it quits and asks Jacob to release him. Jacob demands a blessing in exchange for this release. The angel agrees and asks for Jacob's name. When Jacob tells him, the angel says, "Your name is no longer Jacob, but Yisrael, god-wrestler—for you have wrestled with god and human, and you have prevailed."

Yisrael then asks the angel for his name. The angel says, "Don't you know who I am?" and then vanishes. The implication is that this angel was god, which is why Yisrael exclaims, "I have seen god face to face, and I lived!" (Genesis 32:22–32).

In ancient times, your name represented your essence or core quality. Jacob's name (*Ya'akov* in Hebrew) comes from the word *ekev* (heel) and means "heel-grabber." Jacob was called this because, when he came out of his mother's womb, he was grasping the heel of his twin brother Esau. As a sign of his character, "heel-grabber" implies that Jacob was a usurper of others' power rather than a powerful person in his own right, something the larger story of Jacob and Esau confirms.

Receiving a new name connoted a change in Jacob's character. No longer was he dependent on usurping the power of others. He had come into his own power, a power so strong that it could stand undefeated against god.

This is the first of three qualities associated with the name Yisrael: the strength to wrestle god, which is to say the strength to resist the allure of tribal gods and powers, and to free oneself for the greater task of teshuvah, or God-realization.

As soon as the angel departs, Esau arrives. The old Jacob expected to die at his brother's hand; the new Yisrael, having just held his own against god, may have expected to defeat his brother. Yet as Esau draws near to his brother, something unexpected happens to both men: Esau's anger and Jacob's fear both disappear, and the two brothers fall into each other's arms, weeping in reconciliation (Genesis 33:4). This is the second quality of Yisrael: the capacity for reconciliation with, rather than the defeat of, one's enemies.

After a while, Esau offers to travel at his brother's side. Yisrael turns down the offer, saying, "You walk at the pace of a warrior, while I travel at the pace of the young and the nursing among my family, flocks, and herds. If these were driven hard for even a single day, they would die" (Genesis 33:13). This is the third quality of Yisrael: working to care for and uphold the dignity of the least powerful among us, both human and animal.

All three qualities of Yisrael come at a cost. This is symbolized by the wound Jacob received from the angel. This wound never heals, and Jacob walks with a limp for the rest of his life. It is this limp that keeps Jacob from becoming a warrior like his brother. It is this wound that humbles Jacob, tames the hubris of Jacob the usurper and turns him into Yisrael the god-wrestler.

*

The Jew as god-wrestler is an iconoclast, someone who shatters isms and ideologies and smashes all gods. In this sense, Abraham, Jacob's grandfather—and the founder of Judaism, Christianity, Islam, and Baha'i—was the first god-wrestler.

According to Genesis Rabbah 38, an ancient rabbinic commentary on Abraham's life, Abraham's father Terah was an idol maker. Called away on business, Terah places Abraham (then called Avram) in charge of the idol store.

An older man enters the shop to purchase an idol. Avram asks the man how old he is, and when the man says that he is fifty years old, Avram mocks him: saying, "You are fifty years old, yet you plan to worship a god I baked just yesterday?" The man leaves without making a purchase.

A woman enters the shop later in the day hoping to make an offering to the gods. Not knowing which of the shop's many gods is worthy of her devotion, Avram takes a stick and smashes all the idols but the largest. Then he places the stick in the idol's hand. "Here!" Avram says to the woman. "This is the strongest god—worship him!" Shocked at Avram's behavior, the woman, too, leaves without making a purchase.

Terah returns, only to find all but one idol smashed to pieces. He demands an explanation. Avram says, "A woman entered the shop wishing to make an offering, and the gods warred amongst themselves over who was to receive it. All but this one died in battle." Incensed, Terah shouts at Abram, "These are empty statues! What you say is nonsense!" To which Avram replies, "If you know they are empty statues, why do you worship them?"

*

The result of god-smashing is the opportunity for God-realization, teshuvah: returning to your true nature as a manifesting of the singular, formless, ineffable *YHVH*, the Happening happening as all happening.

The Jew as god-wrestler, iconoclast, and god-smasher doesn't worship god in heaven. Instead, as the Talmudic legend below suggests, they act godly here on Earth:

A group of sages are examining an oven to determine if its innovative design meets their standards for use. Rabbi Eliezer argues that it does, but the other rabbis argue that it doesn't. Seeing that his reasoning isn't persuading his colleagues, Rabbi Eliezer resorts to miracles: "If I am correct, this carob tree will prove it." Immediately, the carob tree leaps from the ground and replants itself several yards away. Unimpressed, the rabbis said, "What does a carob tree know about such matters?"

Rabbi Eliezer then says, "If I am correct, this stream will prove it," and the stream begins to flow backward. The other rabbis again point out that a stream knows nothing of ovens.

Frustrated, Rabbi Eliezer cries out, "If I am correct, the walls of our study hall will prove it." The walls of the study hall begin to collapse, but Rabbi Joshua scolds them for interfering in a rabbinic debate. Out of respect for Rabbi Joshua, the walls do not fall, but out of respect for Rabbi Eliezer, they do not stand upright, either.

Having lost his patience, Rabbi Eliezer finally shouts, "If I am correct, Heaven will prove it."

A voice from Heaven says, "Why are you arguing with Rabbi Eliezer, as it is clear that his position is correct?"

Rabbi Joshua then looks up into the sky and says, "It (the Truth) is not in Heaven! (*lo ba–shamayyim he*, Deuteronomy 30:12). When the sages are debating, even you have no right to interfere."

Hearing this, god laughs and says, "At last, at last, my children have defeated me!" (Talmud, Bava Metzia 59a–b).

∗

Defeating god rather than worshipping god is the work of the Jew as Yisrael. Defeating god frees you from isms and ideologies created by human beings for their own benefit. Defeating god allows you to avoid the pitfalls of tribalism and the gods and clergy that promote it.

∗

Defeating god is essential to the work of teshuvah, God-realization, but it is not an end unto itself. Rather, it is a means to an end: tikkun, repairing the world with justice and compassion. The Jew as Yisrael isn't satisfied with spiritual enlightenment alone. An enlightenment that doesn't lead to worldly justice and compassion is shallow and cheap. This is why Jacob/Yisrael not only wrestles with the powerful but devotes himself to nurturing and protecting the well-being of the powerless as well. This is what it is to be a Jew.

CHAPTER 6

WORLD HEALERS

The real threat to Jewish survival isn't Jew-hatred or inter-marriage, but Jews' own ignorance about why being a Jew matters.

Asking, "Why do Jews matter?" means inquiring into the mission of Judaism. Answering the question in a compelling way means creating a mission for Jews and Judaism that promotes not only the survival of Judaism, but its thriving as well.

*

Think of religions as businesses. Every business has a mission.

The mission of Vedanta Hinduism, for example, is replacing ignorance (*avidya*) with wisdom (*janna*) so that we no longer see ourselves as beings apart from God (*Brahman*, as opposed to the god brahma) but as parts of God.

The mission of Buddhism is the ending of suffering (*dukkah*) by teaching people how to free themselves from endless craving (*trishna*).

The mission of Christianity is salvation through christ.

The mission of Islam is helping people achieve submission to allah through the Five Pillars of Islam.

As long as there are people looking for

wisdom, freedom from suffering, salvation, or surren-
der—Hinduism, Buddhism, Christianity, and Islam will
survive. The same would be true of Judaism: as long as
there are people looking for what Judaism offers, Judaism
will survive. The problem Judaism faces is that Jews are
not always clear about what the mission of Judaism is.
This lack of clarity makes them, and subsequently the
world, ignorant as to why Jews matter.

*

Most Jews, if they think about Judaism at all, think that
Judaism is in the Jew-making business, and that the mission of Judaism is to make Jews more Jewish. This usually
means being more observant of, and more engaged with,
the tribal norms articulated by ancient rabbis and inter-
preted by contemporary ones. This is terribly myopic.

If the purpose of Judaism is to make Jews Jewish—the
epitome of tribalist Judaism—then Judaism has no value
outside the Jewish tribe. It has nothing to offer the world.

And if Judaism has nothing to offer the world, then
Judaism might as well disappear from the world. If there
is no compelling answer to the question, "Why be a Jew?",
then there is no good answer to the question, "Why
bother with Judaism?"

*

From the point of view of Judaism without tribalism, the
mission of Judaism is teshuvah and tikkun: helping return
people to their true nature as a manifesting of God/YHVH
and repairing the world with justice and compassion by
being a blessing to all the families of the earth, human and
otherwise (Genesis 12:3).

Jews are called to be ohr l'goyyim, a "light unto the

nations" Isaiah 49:6). This means shining a light on three fundamental truths: 1) the truth of God/*YHVH* as the Happening happening as all happening (as opposed to god Adonai/Lord, who chose the Jews to be his special people); 2) the truth of humanity as the image of God; and 3) the human obligation to repair the world with justice and compassion by being a blessing. In this way, Judaism ceases to be about Jewish survival and becomes more about the thriving of person and planet. In this way, Judaism ceases to be about making Jews more Jewish and becomes more about making people more just, kind, and humble (Micah 6:8).

If Judaism were a business, our vision of the future wouldn't be a world in which Jews are more engaged with Jewish tradition. It would be a world in which Jews use their traditions, texts, and teachings to help create a civilization where people beat their swords into ploughshares and their spears into pruning hooks; where nation ceases to war against nation; where even the study of war is no longer part of human life; where people live simply beneath their vines and fig trees; where no one threatens another or makes them afraid (Micah 4:3-4); and where people eat simply, drink moderately, work joyously, and love freely (Ecclesiastes 2:24; 4:8–12).

Being a light to the nations is not the same as bringing all the nations to Judaism or making all people Jews. Unlike Christianity and Islam, Judaism doesn't dream of global domination, and Jews are under no obligation to proselytize. On the contrary, the vision of the Jews allows each people to worship god as they see fit (Micah 4:5). This vision assumes that, as Jews shine their light on truth more and more effectively, the gods we invent will be less and less parochial, and more and more in service to the work of tikkun—repairing the world with justice and compassion.

*

If the mission of Judaism is teshuvah and tikkun, then the task of Jewish educators is to teach Jewish texts, traditions, and wisdom as means to God-realization and being a blessing.

Sadly, most Jewish education replaces the mission of teshuvah and tikkun with a tribalist project of getting Jews to adhere to Jewish tradition, according to the standards and understanding of the denomination in which the teaching occurs. Tribalist Jewish education sees Judaism as an end unto itself, rather than a means to a greater and universal end.

Because most Jewish children aren't interested in being Jews for Judaism's sake, the Jewish educator must continually find ways to make Judaism interesting and fun.

If, on the other hand, the focus of Jewish education was on teshuvah and tikkun, there would be no need to make Judaism interesting and fun. It would be intrinsically engaging because it would be about discovering your true Self and being a blessing to all the families of the earth—something to which most people, especially children, are naturally drawn.

*

The goal of Jewish education shouldn't be to raise Jews, but to raise iconoclasts, god-wrestlers, and god-smashers—people who find in Judaism many powerful and compelling tools to enhance their iconoclasm, god-wrestling, and god-smashing.

The goal of Jewish education shouldn't be to train someone to act like a Jew but to think like a Jew. To think like a Jew is to privilege doubt over belief, argument over consensus, and questions over answers. To think like a

Jew is to wrestle with gods, both religious and secular, and to refuse to be satisfied with any answer—especially answers that claim to be the word of some almighty and inerrant god.

Sadly, most Jewish education today isn't devoted to teaching Jews how to think but to telling them what to do.

*

Jewish learning at its best is rooted in *machloket l'shem shamayim*: arguing for the sake of truth in service to teshuvah and tikkun. And machloket l'shem shamayim is rooted in the principle of *elu v'elu d'vrei elohim chayyim*: "These arguments and those arguments, despite their obvious incompatibility, are both the words of the living God," in that they both point to facets of Truth (Talmud, Eruvin 13b).

Elu v'elu means that an educated person isn't someone who knows THE answer, but someone who can hold many answers—even contradictory answers—and still come up with a new question that challenges them all.

Since Truth is always beyond our capacity to formulate in words, machloket l'shem shamayim is an endless process of building up ideas, isms, and ideologies, testing them against our mission as Jews, and daring to demolish them if and when they fail to further that mission. What matters—or what should matter—is continuity not with the Jewish past but with the Jewish mission.

*

Elu v'elu and machloket l'shem shamayyim require dialogue. For this reason, Jewish learning at its best is done in *chavruta*, gatherings of two or more study partners whose job is to deepen the dialogue by sharpening the questions the partners ask.

Unfortunately, this style of learning is rare today. Instead, most Jewish learning happens in the setting of a classroom, with a teacher and multiple students, and where the task of the teacher is to impart knowledge and the task of the student is to repeat what is taught.

The difference between these two learning styles is profound. In the teacher-student setting, the teacher typically expounds, and the student typically memorizes what the teacher expounds. In chavruta-style learning, there is no teacher-student hierarchy, and no one is presumed to have THE answer to a given problem. Rather, each partner does their best to sharpen their analysis of the issue; prepare cogent arguments in defense of their position; listen to the arguments of their peers; and then push one another beyond their respective arguments to discover new insights that none could have imagined alone. The role of the teacher in such settings is to see where a group of learners has stalled in their arguments and to introduce new texts and alternative arguments to keep the discussion moving.

The aim of conventional Jewish education is to achieve or impose consensus. The aim of elu v'elu, machloket l'shem shamayyim, and chavruta is to sharpen the mind of each partner. As Rabbi Yochanan said of his partner Reish Lakish, "Whenever I would pose an idea, he would find twenty-four flaws in my reasoning. I would then find twenty-four solutions to the problems he raised. Eventually, in this way, the subject we were discussing would clarify itself in our minds" (Talmud, Bava Metzia 84a).

*

The mission of Judaism is teshuvah and tikkun—and because it is, I am drawn to it. It is at the heart of why I call myself a Jew.

One of the best expressions of this mission was articulated by the French Jewish writer Edmund Fleg (1874–1963):

> I am a Jew because Judaism demands no abdication of the mind.
>
> I am a Jew because Judaism asks every possible sacrifice of my life.
>
> I am a Jew because wherever there are tears and suffering, the Jew weeps.
>
> I am a Jew because whenever the cry of despair is heard, the Jew hopes.
>
> I am a Jew because the message of Judaism is the oldest and the newest.
>
> I am a Jew because the promise of Judaism is a universal promise.
>
> I am a Jew because, for the Jew, the world is unfinished; people will complete it.
>
> I am a Jew because, for the Jew, humanity is unfinished; we are still creating it.
>
> I am a Jew because Judaism places human dignity above all things, even Judaism itself.
>
> I am a Jew because Judaism places human dignity within the oneness of God.

*

To Fleg's wonderful list I would add the following:

> I am a Jew because I find in Judaism a way to teshuvah and tikkun.

I am a Jew because I find in Judaism tools for being a blessing.

I am a Jew because I find in Judaism a community that sharpens my questions and questions my answers.

I am a Jew because I find in Judaism a call to wrestle with the powerful.

I am a Jew because I find in Judaism the challenge to empower the powerless.

I am a Jew because I find being a Jew to be a challenge demanding nothing less than the best of which I am capable: physically, emotionally, intellectually, and spiritually.

CHAPTER 7

LAMED-VAVNIKS

Sixteen hundred years ago, the Babylonian Jewish sage Rabbi Abaye (d. 337 CE) revealed a secret which was, even then, centuries old.

Abaye taught that, at any given moment, there are at least thirty-six (*lamed-vav* in Hebrew) women and men actively engaged in being blessings to all the families of the earth (Talmud, Sanhedrin 97b). Because of the efforts of these thirty-six people, human civilization withstands the impulse to implode under the weight of its own ignorance, arrogance, and greed.

Tribalist Judaism focuses on making Jews Jewish. In contrast, Judaism without tribalism focuses on making people *lamed-vavniks.*

The term lamed-vavnik comes from the two Hebrew letters that comprise the number thirty-six: lamed (thirty) and vav (six). The Yiddish suffix *nik* is like the English suffix *ers*; lamed-vavniks are literally thirty-sixers.

A lamed-vavnik is someone who takes up the mission of teshuvah and tikkun. If a lamed-vavnik identifies as a Jew, they are a Jewish lamed-vavnik. If they choose not to identify as a Jew, they are still a lamed-vavnik.

*

The Hasidic sage Menachem Mendel of Kotzk (1787-1859) points directly to the fundamental insight of the lamed-vavnik:

> If I am I because I am I; and You are you because you are you; then I am I and you are you.
>
> But if I am I because You are you; and You are you because I am I; then You are not only you and I am not only I.

*

The first statement—"If I am I because I am I; and You are you because you are you"—is the mindset Judaism calls *mochin d'katnut*, narrow mind, the mind given to self and selfishness. The second statement—"If I am I because you are you; and You are you because I am I"—is the mindset Judaism calls *mochin d'gadlut*, spacious mind, the mind given to Self and selflessness. Mochin d'gadlut knows that I am I only in relation to you, and you are you only in relationship to me—and I am not separate from you and you are not separate from me.

With this knowing comes a deeper realization that each "I" and each "You" arises from the dynamic interconnectedness of all life in, with, and as *YHVH*, the Happening happening as all happening. With this knowing also comes an unshakable commitment to see to the welfare of every *I* and every *you*.

The lamed-vavnik, Jewish or otherwise, doesn't try to erase narrow mind, but places it in the greater context of spacious mind: I am not ONLY I, and you are not ONLY you.

*

A jigsaw puzzle provides us with a sound analogy here. You and I and all beings are like pieces of the puzzle. While each piece is unique, on its own it is also irrelevant. Only in relation with all the other pieces and the puzzle as a whole does each piece become meaningful. Interacting in this way doesn't rob you of your individuality or value but actualizes them. Mochin d'katnut, narrow mind, sees only separate pieces. Spacious mind sees the pieces only in relation to the whole. Both minds are necessary.

This what the mid-first-century BCE Babylonian Jewish sage Hillel taught when he said:

> If I am not for myself, who will be for me?
> If I am only for myself, what am I?
> If not now, when? (Pirke Avot 1:14)

"If I am not for myself, who will be for me?" Hillel is not discussing self-esteem here. The "self" to which he refers isn't the ego, but the Self: your innate capacity to know all beings as happenings of *YHVH*. You need to realize this Self; no one else can do it for you. Your first challenge as a lamed-vavnik is to open narrow mind to spacious mind and realize the interdependence of all life in the aliveness of *YHVH*.

"If I am only for myself, what am I?" It is easy to read this as an admonition against selfishness—which it is. But it can just as easily be understood as an admonition against selflessness. If I am only for Self—that is, if I am so absorbed in inner mystic revelry that the world and the world's suffering appears illusory to me—then I am irrelevant. My turning inward (teshuvah) must be balanced by my turning outward (tikkun), repairing person to person and person to planet. Done rightly, being for your Self leads to being for all selves (Leviticus 19:18).

"If not now, when?" Now is this very moment, however it presents itself. Now is every moment, with all its conflict, confusion, and uncertainty. When is a fantasy time of perfect peace, clarity, and certainty. You—and I, and everyone else—are always in the perfectly imperfect Now. You may prefer to put off engaging with *Now* until some utopian *When* arrives, but because it is always Now, that When never comes.

*

For most of the last sixteen hundred years, Abaye's reference to the number thirty-six was taken literally. People thought that in every generation there are always thirty-six women and men who are awake to, in, and as *YHVH*. These thirty-six human beings are dedicated to being a blessing to all the families of the earth, each in their own way. Reading Abaye this way lets us off the hook. After all, there is no way that I am or ever could be a lamed-vavnik.

A more fruitful and personally challenging way to understand Abaye's teaching is to understand the number thirty-six metaphorically. *Gematria*, Hebrew numerology, applies a numerical value to each Hebrew letter in order to reveal hidden meanings in Hebrew words. The Hebrew word *chai* (life), for example, carries the numerical sum of eighteen (*chet*/8 + *yud*/10). Abaye's use of thirty-six points not only to the minimum number of awakened people needed to sustain human civilization and the flourishing of planet Earth, but also to the double life (twice chai: 18 x 2) lived by those who do the work of being a blessing. Those who choose to be a blessing live both for themselves and for the world. Indeed, they no longer imagine that they are other than the world. In this sense, they live double chai—twice eighteen, or thirty-six.

*

Abaye believed that lamed-vavniks live every minute of their lives as a blessing. I disagree. In my experience, people step into and out of moments of being a blessing.

Abaye also believed that when one lamed-vavnik dies, another is born, thus maintaining the necessary minimum number of thirty-six. My own sense is that, while there are always at least thirty-six people on the planet who are being a blessing at any given moment, they are not necessarily the same people from moment to moment. As one person steps out of the lamed-vavnik role, another steps in.

Judaism without tribalism calls you to step into being a lamed-vavnik as often as you can. And every moment is an opportunity for each of us to take that step.

PART THREE
JUDAISM

CHAPTER 8

BEYOND TRIBALISM

There is no word for "religion" in Judaism. The term we use is *da'at*, which means knowledge. A religious person is called a *da'ati*, "one who knows." What one knows is *YHVH* manifesting all Reality.

Knowing is not the same as believing. Believing is an act of affirming as true something that cannot be proven to be true. Knowing is a direct experience of truth itself.

*

Many Jews believe that the creator god of the universe chose the Jews from among all the peoples of the earth. This god made the Jews his special people and gave them his one true revelation, Torah, as well as the deed to the promised land in perpetuity. This is tribalism.

*

Judaism without tribalism is Judaism without god, but with God. God is *YHVH*, the Happening happening as all happening.

Unlike god, *YHVH* doesn't choose one people over others, or write books, or dabble in real estate.

YHVH is Reality itself. What Jews call *YHVH*, Hindus call Brahman, Buddhists call Dharmakaya, Taoists call

---

Tao, Muslims call Al-Mutakabbir, and Christians call the Godhead. The God to which all of these names point is not the god of any one tribe created for the benefit of that tribe. This God is the source and substance of all Reality, of which each thing is a part.

*

An awareness of *YHVH* happening as all happening kindles a deep love for all things. In Jews with this awareness, this love shapes our understanding of our stories so that they guide us in being a light unto all the nations. At the heart of this awareness is compassion.

Hillel (110 BCE–10 CE) was once approached by a man who mockingly challenged him to teach the entire Torah—what was by then already a two-thousand-year-old tradition—while the man stood on one foot. Hillel unhesitatingly replied, "That which is hateful to you, do not do to another. That is the entire Torah. All the rest is commentary. Now, go and study it!" (Talmud Shabbat 31a).

Jews are so familiar with this teaching that we often overlook its radical nature. When Hillel says that "all the rest is commentary," he means that all Jewish texts, traditions, teachings, and practices serve compassion. According to Hillel's understanding of Judaism, then, any Jewish text, tradition, teaching, or practice that does not help you become more compassionate is not authentically Jewish.

Where did Hillel derive this notion of Torah from? The saying "That which is hateful to you do not do to another" doesn't appear in the Hebrew Bible. The closest we come in Torah is "Love your neighbor as yourself" (Leviticus 19:18). But if Hillel meant to say that, he would have said it.

Hillel didn't cite Leviticus 19:18 because of the first half of the verse: "Do not hold a grudge against members of your people." The words "your people" make it clear that the neighbor in the second half of the verse was your Jewish neighbor. But love your Jewish neighbor" was too tribal for Hillel. He wanted a Torah that spoke to all of humankind, not just to Jews.

Hillel taught Judaism without tribalism.

*

The central theological insight of Judaism without tribalism is the nonduality of God: *YHVH echad*, "God is one" (Deuteronomy 6:4).

Mainstream Judaism understands "God is one" to mean that the Jewish god is numerically one—rather than three, like the god of the Christian Trinity, or thirty-three, like the gods of Vedic Hinduism. But as my rebbe Zalman Schachter-Shalomi (1924–2014) taught me in the name of the Alter Rebbe, Schneur Zalman of Liadi (1745–1813), if the meaning of *echad* is that god is one and not two, then we wouldn't need to recite this affirmation multiple times each day.

Echad is not about being one rather than two, but about oneness itself, or nonduality: the greater whole within which all numbers exist. In reciting "God is one" multiple times each day, we remind ourselves that the seeming duality of things, which appear separate and apart from one another, is actually part of a greater nonduality, in which everything is a part of *YHVH*, and nothing is apart from *YHVH*.

Think of a magnet. The magnet is singular, yet it manifests as two equal and opposite poles. What is true of a magnet is true of *YHVH*: an infinite whole manifesting all opposites.

The magnet doesn't choose to be one pole or the other but is, by its very nature, both poles together. In the same way, *YHVH* doesn't discriminate between opposites, but manifests as all of them: "I manifest light and dark, I create good and evil; I *YHVH* do all things" (Isaiah 45:7).

*

Torah refers to the nonduality of *YHVH* as *ain od milvado*: "Know this day and take it to heart that *YHVH* is God permeating heaven and earth—ain od milvado, there is nothing else" (Deuteronomy 4:39); "I am the first and I am the last, and besides Me there is nothing at all (ain od milvado)" [Isaiah 44:6].

Every living thing is an extension of an infinite, nondual, dynamic, and ever-evolving aliveness (chiut) that is *YHVH*: "The whole cosmos is alive with the energy of God" (Isaiah 6:3); "I *YHVH* fill the heavens and the earth" (Jeremiah 23:24). *YHVH* fills the cosmos the way an ocean fills its waves and a magnet fills its positive and negative poles.

Nature is a happening of *YHVH* in the same way that waves are a waving of the ocean: "The cosmos declares the energy of God" (Psalm 19:2).

The more fully we understand the natural world, the more deeply we understand the interdependence of all life in the greater aliveness (chiut) of *YHVH*. And the more we understand this interdependence, the better we can fulfill our mission to serve and protect life (Genesis 2:15), and to be a blessing to all the living (Genesis 12:3).

*

Because everything is God, you too are God.

Just as a wave is nothing but the ocean waving it, so you are nothing but *YHVH* happening as you.

God manifests as opposites, so you manifest as opposites. These include mochin d'katnut and mochin d'gadlut—the narrow mind of self and the spacious mind of Self. They also include *yetzer ha-rah* and *yetzer ha-tov*—the capacity for self-expression and self-care, and the capacity for Self-realization and other-care.

Mochin d'katnut honors difference and celebrates diversity. Mochin d'gadlut knows all diversity as manifestings of *YHVH*—as chiut, or aliveness.

Yetzer ha-rah empowers you to pursue your own specialness and uniqueness—to fall in love, raise a family, start a business or build a career, and care for self and those most dear to you. Yetzer ha-tov empowers you to help others do the same (Talmud, Berachot 61b).

Like the two poles of a magnet, mochin d'katnut and mochin d'gadlut, along with yetzer ha-rah and yetzer ha-tov, need each other.

When we are out of touch with spacious mind and yetzer ha-tov, narrow mind is trapped in a selfish, zero-sum worldview of "us against them," in which the success of one always appears to be at the expense of another.

When we are out of touch with narrow mind and yetzer ha-rah, spacious mind is lost in a selfless and world-denying ecstasy, where the needs and welfare of each part is lost in the awesomeness of the Whole.

Only when mochin d'katnut and mochin d'gadlut, and yetzer ha-rah and yetzer ha-tov are in dynamic balance, each yielding to the other as the moment demands, can you see the world as a celebration of "all of us together," where the success and welfare of each depends on the success and welfare of all.

As noted earlier, Hillel spoke of this balance when he said, "If I am not for myself, who will be for me? If I am only for myself, what am I? And if not now, when?" (Pirke Avot 1:14).

If you are not for yourself—that is, if you do not cultivate mochin d'katnut and yetzer ha-rah—you will have little impact on the world. But if you are only for yourself, and not for others as well—that is, if you do not cultivate mochin d'gadlut and yetzer ha-tov—you will not live up to your human potential as the image of God.

Balancing our narrow and spacious minds is a continuous task, taking place in this and every moment. If not now, when? Balancing narrow and spacious minds is the deep spiritual work of Judaism without tribalism.

CHAPTER 9

TURNING TORAH

Torah is a feminine noun meaning "teaching," and is the earliest anthology of Jewish insights into the nature of life and how best to live it.

Torah is a "Tree of Life to all who embrace her" (Proverbs 3:18)—and embracing Torah means engaging with her to reveal her central message. That message, as Hillel understood it, is: What is hateful to you do not do to another (Shabbat 31a). In other words, the central teaching of Torah is to live a life and create a world founded in justice and compassion.

A Judaism without tribalism accepts as true only those Torah teachings that promote justice and compassion. Everything else we understand to be the pronouncements of tribal leaders in search of power.

Both, however, are worthy of study. We study the Torah of justice and compassion to see the best that we are capable of. We study the Torah of power to see the worst.

*

Torah was originally an oral teaching passed on from generation to generation: "Speak words of Torah to your children. Speak words of Torah when sitting at home, walking on the road, when you lay down to sleep at night, and when you rise up again in the morning" (Deuteronomy

6:7). Torah was already a thousand years old before being cast in its final written form, sometime between 450 and 350 BCE.

The advantage of an oral teaching is that it is fluid and adaptable to different times and situations. The speakers of Torah can "remember" Torah in different ways, and thus keep Torah flexible and focused on compassion.

The disadvantage of a written Torah is that it too easily becomes fixed, stale, and outmoded. To keep the written Torah fluid, the early rabbis invented ways of deliberately misreading the written text so that it yields new meanings. We call this creative reading and reinterpreting turning. The term comes from the first-century CE sage Ben Bag Bag, who said of Torah, "Turn her and turn her, for everything is in her" (Pirke Avot 5:21).

*

Turning Torah enables us to avoid falling into the trap of literalism.

Turning Torah is more an act of literary imagination than textual fealty. This is facilitated by the fact that the printed Torah lacks vowels.

Someone who learns to read Torah learns the conventions regarding what vowels to read and where. Someone who learns how to turn Torah discovers new meaning in her by breathing new vowels into her.

For example, take Reb Nachman of Breslov's (1772–1810) deliberate misreading of "Love your neighbor as yourself" (Leviticus 19:18). The Hebrew word for "neighbor" in Torah is spelled with two consonants, *resh* and *ayin*, and is pronounced *reah*. Reb Nachman saw that the same two consonants can just as easily be pronounced *rah*, which is the Hebrew word for evil. From this shift of vowels, Reb Nachman derived the teaching that you cannot love your neighbor as yourself until you first love your capacity for evil as a part of yourself. If you don't accept your own capacity for evil, you will project your evil onto your neighbor, and this will make loving that neighbor all the more difficult.

*

Another method for keeping Torah fluid is gematria, Hebrew numerology.

The Hebrew language has no numerals. Instead, each letter of the *alef-bet* carries a numerical value, and so does double duty as both letter and number. *Alef* (a) equals the number 1, *bet* (b) equals the number 2, and so on.

Every Hebrew word of Torah can be read as an arithmetic sum, and words that share the same value arithmetically can be understood as synonyms. Gematria thus yields multitudes of deliberate misreadings of Torah that are philosophically and spiritually valid—in that they lead to teshuvah and tikkun—though not necessarily linguistically sound.

For example, the Hebrew word *elohim*, usually translated as god, has the arithmetic value of 86: alef/1 + *lamed*/30 + *hey*/5 + *yud*/10 + *mem*/40. Using gematria as our tool for turning Torah, we find that the Hebrew word *hateva*, "nature," also adds up to 86: hey/5 + *tet*/9 + bet/2 + ayin/70. Because elohim and *hateva* share the same value, they can be read as synonyms. Doing so yields a radically different—yet no less legitimate—opening verse of Torah. Rather than the conventional "In the beginning, god created the heavens and the earth," our gematria turning reveals a very different revelation: In the beginning, nature created the heavens and earth (Genesis 1:1).

The point isn't that one of these readings is true and the other false, but that both are true at the same time.

This is the pedagogical principle of elu v'elu mentioned earlier.

Turning Torah liberates Torah from the literal to free the human imagination for the work of teshuvah and tikkun.

Gematria strikes some people as liberating and deeply creative, and others as bizarre and off-putting. If you find gematria to be liberating and creative, use it to turn Torah yourself. If you find it off-putting or bizarre, reject it and turn Torah using other tools. You'll find two such tools below.

*

A third tool for turning Torah is called PaRDeS, an acronym meaning "garden, orchard, or paradise." PaRDes is comprised of the first letter of four levels of Torah turning: *Peshat* ("simple"), the literal reading of the text; *Remez* ("hint"), in which problems that arise from a literal reading are used as hints pointing toward a deeper, nonliteral reading; *Drash* ("investigate"), in which you use your imagination to create new meanings from deeper, nonliteral readings; and *Sod* ("secret"), in which you go beyond ordinary imagination to intuit radically new insights. Ideally, these insights involve the nature of life and how best to live it as a blessing to all the families of the earth.

One classic application of PaRDeS is in the story of Abraham's near sacrifice of Isaac. As Abraham, Isaac, and the family's servants prepare to ascend the mountain where Abraham has been commanded to sacrifice Isaac, Abraham orders the servants to stay behind. "My son and I will climb the mountain, there we will worship, and then we will return to you" (Genesis 22:5). That is the literal (peshat) reading of Torah.

The hint (remez) that there is more to this story is found in Abraham saying that both he and Isaac will return to the servants—even though Abraham knows that he is supposed to kill his son on the mountain peak.

Using your imagination, you investigate (drash) possible reasons for Abraham saying what he said. Perhaps he said it to spare Isaac's feelings, or to keep Isaac from resisting the climb to the mountain's summit. Perhaps he said it because he had no intention of killing his son, god or no god. Or perhaps ... what other reasons appear in your mind?

There is no single answer in Judaism, only the invitation to hone your capacity to imagine more.

As you do this, you might uncover some hidden meaning (sod) that no one has yet imagined. What this might be, only you will know. However, if you like, you can then share, discuss, or debate that new meaning with others.

＊

Another way to keep Torah fluid is called Four Worlds Turning. The four worlds are the four dimensions of human existence: assiyah (the physical), yetzirah (the emotional), beriah (the intellectual), and atzilut (the spiritual).

As you turn a Torah teaching, notice how your body responds. Does it tighten or soften? Notice how your heart responds. Is it filled with love or fear? Notice how your rational mind responds. Does it see value of the teaching as a tool of justice and compassion, or does it have to rationalize the teaching because it violates Hillel's Torah of compassion? Notice how your spirit responds. Does the teaching enlarge your capacity to be a blessing, or does it diminish or restrict it?

Teachings that soften the body, fill the heart with love, open the mind, and deepen the spirit are part of Hillel's Torah.

One example of the Four Worlds Turning comes from my own rebbe, Reb Zalman Schachter Shalomi. He turned Leviticus 20:13, which says that "a man shall not lie with another man as he does with a woman, for if they do they have committed an abomination and shall be put to death."

The original author of this text clearly wanted to outlaw male homosexuality. (Torah says nothing about lesbian sexual intimacy.)

But Reb Zalman noticed that reading this passage tightened his body, closed his heart, demanded some rationale to excuse what was clearly a heinous teaching, and left him spiritually weakened rather than empowered. So, he turned the text this way: A man should not be sexually intimate with another man while pretending this other man is a woman. In other words, your intimacy with another should be based on the integrity of both partners. The abomination is lying to oneself and lying to your partner. The penalty is death of your spirit, in that denying your own sexuality is dying to your own truth and authenticity.

*

I'm always surprised when people try to make Torah, or the entire Bible, into a children's book. Torah is not a children's book. It is a book of parables and stories for exploring the light and dark sides of the human psyche, written by and for adults. When we dumb down Torah so that it meets the needs of preschoolers, we damage Torah in our minds. Then, as adults, we fail to find her compelling.

CHAPTER 10

DAYS OF REFLECTION

Haggim (Jewish holy days) are question marks: moments of deep inquiry and wonder. At the heart of each holy day, or *hag*, is a question to be asked and pondered, though never definitively answered.

Judaism has many different days of holiness, celebration, and commemoration each year, so let us focus here only on the ones that are most well-known. (Shabbat, the Sabbath, is perhaps the most well-known of all—but because it is celebrated fifty-two times each year as part of the natural rhythm of each week, I'll discuss it in Chapter 13: Halacha: The Way We Walk.)

*

ROSH HASHANAH

Rosh HaShanah is the anniversary of humanity's birth. This holy day calls us to recommit to the work of teshuvah: returning to our true nature as the image and likeness of *YHVH* (Genesis 1:26). As such, the core question of Rosh HaShanah is, Who am I?

The answer is that you are a manifesting of *YHVH*, who is charged with caring for the earth (Genesis 2:15) and being a blessing to all the families of the earth (Genesis 12:3).

The process of returning to our true nature brings with it a host of other questions:

How am I liberating myself from ignorance? Where am I failing to do so? How and where am I doing justly, acting kindly, and walking humbly? Where am I failing to do so? How am I leading the world beyond conflict to harmony, beyond fear to love, and beyond scarcity to abundance? Where am I failing to do so?

This inquiry is expressed in a liturgical poem of self-inquiry known as *Unetaneh Tokef* ("We ascribe holiness to this day"), which is recited only on Rosh HaShanah and Yom Kippur. Here is the translation I use:

> On Rosh HaShanah we question, on Yom Kippur we inquire:
>
> Who shall live, and who shall die?
>
> Who shall live the fulness of each day, and who shall live as if already dead?
>
> Who shall be sustained by the waters of compassion, and who consumed by the fires of rage?
>
> Who shall live by peace, and who by violence?
>
> Who shall be fed by friendship, and who shall starve for lack of love?
>
> Who shall drown in life's storms, and who shall learn to ride them out?
>
> Who shall be impoverished by endless desire, and who shall be enriched by simplicity and joy?

*

Playing with the vowels of the Hebrew words *rosh*/head and *shanah*/year, Reb Nachman of Breslov (1772-1810) read shanah as *shinui* (change) and taught that the work of Rosh HaShanah was to change your head and shift from mochin d'katnut, the narrow mind of self, to the greater Reality in which it rests: mochin d'gadlut, the spacious mind of Self.

Opening mochin d'katnut to mochin d'gadlut is how you can overcome what Albert Einstein called the "optical delusion of consciousness" that alienates you from others. Your task on Rosh HaShanah is to free yourself from this delusion and widen your circle of compassion to include all living creatures, as well as nature as a whole.

Being free from delusion, and widening your circle of compassion, is described in Rosh HaShanah celebrations as being inscribed in the Book of Life. To do this, you spend the month leading up to Rosh HaShanah in a self-emptying exercise of humbly asking forgiveness from all those with whom you come into regular contact: family, friends, coworkers, neighbors, and so on. During the eight days between Rosh HaShanah and Yom Kippur you cultivate the Thirteen Attributes of Godliness, which we will explore in Chapter 13.

*

Perhaps the most well-known Rosh HaShanah ritual is the blowing of the *shofar*, or ram's horn. The shofar is sounded in four blasts:

> 1) *tekiah*: the single note of teshuvah (return), reminding us of our original unity as the image and likeness of *YHVH*.

> 2) *shevarim*: three short notes, representing the loss of unity through ignorance, arrogance, and fear.

> 3) *teruah*: nine staccato notes, representing the shattering of the world caused by anger, self-pity,

self-righteousness, self-obsession, xenophobia, tribalism, ignorance, arrogance, and fear.

4) *tekiah tedolah*: the "Great Blast"—one long and final note of tikkun (repair)—which reminds us of our true nature and sets us back on the road to being a blessing.

＊

YOM KIPPUR

Yom Kippur is a day of fasting and personal and communal soul searching. On Yom Kippur, we focus on the question, Why am I here?

We fast not to punish the body (after all, we are only skipping one day's breakfast and lunch), but to focus the mind to better explore our question. This is why fasting is associated with revelation and prophecy (Exodus 34:28; I Samuel 28:20), as well as with repentance (Jonah 3:5).

Asking this question requires us to affirm our commitment to tikkun, repairing the world with justice and compassion. It also requires us to acknowledge where and how we have failed to live out this commitment, both as individuals and as a community. This is a first step toward overcoming these failures and setting ourselves and our society on a path toward justice, compassion, and peace. We do this in two ways: through *Kol Nidre* and through *Al Chet*.

Kol Nidre ("All Vows") was a sixth-century rabbinic creation that was designed to make null and void all vows of allegiance to Christianity (and later Islam) that Jews were forced to make under a threat of death. Over time, Kol Nidre was applied to render null and void all rash vows made in moments of extreme duress. To this we now add any and all false or harmful beliefs that undermine the thriving of self and other.

Reciting Kol Nidre is an act of self-liberation from everything that has kept you from being a blessing. Here is my preferred translation:

> I publicly renounce all vows and oaths I have made from last Yom Kippur to this Yom Kippur that bind me to harmful or hurtful behaviors, ideas, and organizations, and that inhibit my efforts to be a blessing to all the families of the earth. Let them all be relinquished and abandoned, null and void, neither firm nor established.
>
> May all vows and oaths I may make from this Yom Kippur to the next be in service to teshuvah and tikkun: returning to my true self as a manifesting of God, and to my highest calling: being a blessing by repairing the world with justice and compassion.

*

Al Chet ("Our Sins") is a communal confession of any actions we engaged in, supported, or permitted that worked against the wellbeing of person and planet. Each verse of the Al Chet begins with "For the sins we committed against life and the flourishing of life…"

Among the sins we traditionally confess and seek to outgrow are deception, disrespect, lying, slander, cheating, pride, impudence, stirring up hatred. To these I add the sins of racism, misogyny, irresponsible use of natural resources, and the degradation of any humans, any animals, and nature as a whole.

*

SUKKOT

Five days after Yom Kippur is Sukkot, the Feast of Booths, marking the autumn harvest (Leviticus 23:40). We celebrate Sukkot by building *sukkot* ("booths"): fragile dwellings that are open to the elements and decorated with the bounty of the season. These decorated booths remind us that life's fragility doesn't preclude happiness, creativity, and joy.

We gather with family and friends in a *sukkah* (the singular form of sukkot) to eat, reconnect with our place in nature, and turn the biblical book of Ecclesiastes. This book asks the question at the heart of Sukkot: How shall we live in a fragile and forever dying world?

Ecclesiastes opens with the affirmation *hevel havalim... hakol hevel* (Ecclesiastes 1:2). This is often translated as "vanities of vanities, all is vanity." But the word *hevel* actually means "breath" or "vapor," and is best understood as "impermanence." Ecclesiastes teaches us how to live meaningful, loving, and joyous lives in the midst of uncertainty and impermanence.

The central ritual of Sukkot is the waving of the *lulav* and *etrog*. The lulav is a palm frond with sprigs of willow and myrtle attached to it, symbolizing the masculine energies of life. The etrog is a citrus fruit native to the Middle East; it symbolizes the feminine energies of life. We hold the lulav and etrog together in two hands, and wave them in the six directions—east, south, west, north, up and down—to give thanks for nature's bounty; to recommit ourselves to protect and serve her flourishing (Genesis 2:15); and to unite all opposites in the greater harmony of the whole, of which each life is a part.

*

SIMCHAT TORAH

Coming immediately after Sukkot, the holy day of *Simchat Torah* ("Rejoicing in Torah") celebrates the centrality of literacy and literature in Jewish life. It also marks the conclusion of one year-long cycle of Torah turning and the beginning of the next. As the Israeli author Amos Oz wrote, "Ours is not a blood line but a text line."

Centuries ago, Muslims began calling the Jews "the people of the book." It is more accurate to say that we are a people of books: we write them, read them, and argue over them in a ceaseless celebration of the human capacity to think new thoughts and create new insights. It is not an exaggeration to say that we Jews are obsessed with books.

So, we set aside one day a year to celebrate our love of books, represented by our most precious book, Torah, the Five Books of Moses. During Simchat Torah, you ask yourself this question: What is the state of my Jewish literacy?

On this holy day, we also hug Torah and dance with her around the sanctuary, knowing that "she is a Tree of Life to those who embrace her" (Proverbs 3:18). We turn her and turn her, knowing that great wisdom resides with her (Pirke Avot 5:21). We argue over her for the sake of heaven (machloket l'shem shemayim), in order to deepen our understanding of and commitment to, Hillel's Torah of justice and compassion. And as soon as we chant the final verses of Deuteronomy, which speak of the death of Moses, we immediately chant the opening verses of Genesis, celebrating new birth and affirming that our love of Torah and literacy will never cease.

*

HANUKKAH

Originally, Hanukkah ("dedication") was a celebration of the second-century BCE military victory of the Maccabees over the Greco-Syrians, and the eight-day rededication of the Temple in Jerusalem that followed.

But the early rabbis were uncomfortable with celebrating a war. So they reimagined Hanukkah by shifting its focus away from a victorious war to the miracle of a single day's worth of oil burning for the entire eight days needed to rededicate the Temple.

To support this new meaning of Hanukkah, the rabbis instituted the ritual of lighting the *hanukkiah* (the Hanukkah menorah) for eight nights. On the first night, two candles are lit: the shammash or attendant candle, which is used to light the other candles, plus one candle to represent the first of the eight nights. Each evening, for the next seven evenings, another candle is added until, on the eighth night, nine candles burn. Here are the blessings I recite on each night:

> First night: We kindle this light in honor of Hope. May we never abandon ourselves to despair.

> Second night: We kindle this light in honor of Action. If we want justice, we must do justly.

> Third night: We kindle this light in honor of Nature. May we never forget our role as her caretaker (Genesis 2:5).

> Fourth night: We kindle this light in honor of Unity. May we come to see each and every person, animal, and thing as expressions of the One.

Fifth night: We kindle this light in honor of Knowledge. May we cultivate intuition and reason in service to truth.

Sixth night: We kindle this light in honor of Kindness. May we be a source of comfort and compassion to all we meet.

Seventh night: We kindle this light in honor of Awareness, being present to the One who is all.

Eighth night: We kindle this light in honor of Heroines and Heroes, ordinary people daring to do extraordinary things.

The true miracle of Hanukkah isn't the rabbinic fiction that the oil lasted for eight days but that the Jews lighted the oil at all, knowing that it could not last the required period. In other words, Hanukkah is a celebration of daring and chutzpah: acting rightly without any surety that the desired end can be achieved.

Thus, the inner spiritual work of Hanukkah is to examine your life in light (pun intended) of the question this holy day poses: Where are you daring to do the impossible in service to being a blessing?

✳

TU B'SHVAT

Tu b'Shvat, literally the fifteenth day of the month of *Shvat*, is called Rosh HaShanah *La'ilannot*, the "New Year of the Trees." Originally, Tu b'Shvat was the day on which people calculated the age of fruit-bearing trees. In ancient times, this mattered because produce from fruit trees younger than three years old was not taxed, while produce from fruit trees three years of age and older was. Today Tu b'Shvat has become Jewish Arbor Day, when Jews around the world plant trees, both locally and in Israel.

The question Tu b'Shvat poses is this: Is your relationship with nature one of I–It or I–Thou? The choice, and the specific wording, come from the Jewish philosopher Martin Buber (1878–1965). Buber taught that there are only two ways to engage with the world: I–It and I–Thou.

Put simply, I–It is the perspective of mochin d'katnut, narrow mind. This is the limited self-focused awareness that sees itself apart from the larger world and grants itself the right to use the larger world for its own benefit. Mochin d'katnut grants exalted status to the individual self—the "I"—but treats everything else in the world as an object to be used, exploited, or manipulated.

I–Thou is the perspective of mochin d'gadlut, spacious mind. This is unlimited Self-awareness that sees itself as a part of the larger world and seeks to engage with the world as a blessing.

My own celebration of Tu b'Shvat includes sitting outside near a tree and contemplating these words of Martin Buber:

> I consider a tree.
>
> I can look on it as a picture: stiff column in a shock of light, or splash of green shot with the delicate blue and silver of the background.
>
> I can perceive it as movement: flowing veins on clinging, pressing pith, suck of the roots, breathing of the leaves, ceaseless commerce with earth and air—and the obscure growth itself.
>
> I can classify it in a species and study it as a type in its structure and mode of life.
>
> I can subdue its actual presence and form so

sternly that I recognize it only as an expression of law—of the laws in accordance with which a constant opposition of forces is continually adjusted, or of those in accordance with which the component substances mingle and separate.

I can dissipate it and perpetuate it in number, in pure numerical relation.

In all this the tree remains my object, occupies space and time, and has its nature and constitution.

It can, however, also come about, if I have both will and grace, that in considering the tree I become bound up in relation to it. The tree is now no longer It. I have been seized by the power of exclusiveness.

To effect this, it is not necessary for me to give up any of the ways in which I consider the tree. There is nothing from which I would have to turn my eyes away in order to see, and no knowledge that I would have to forget. Rather is everything, picture and movement, species and type, law and number, indivisibly united in this event.

Everything belonging to the tree is in this: its form and structure, its colors and chemical composition, its intercourse with the elements and with the stars, are all present in a single whole.

The tree is no impression, no play of my imagination, no value depending on my mood; but it is bodied over against me and has to do with me, as I with it —only in a different way.

Let no attempt be made to sap the strength from the meaning of the relation: relation is mutual.

The tree will have a consciousness, then, similar to our own? Of that I have no experience. But do you wish, through seeming to succeed in it with yourself, once again to disintegrate that which cannot be disintegrated? I encounter no soul or dryad of the tree, but the tree itself.

(Martin Buber, *I and Thou*, trans. Ronald Gregor Smith, [New York: Scribner Books, 2000], 22–23)

*

PURIM

Purim celebrates the survival of the Jews against overwhelming odds. The question at the heart of this holy day is: How much will you risk for justice?

Purim is based on the biblical book of Esther, a fictional account of a Jewish woman who becomes Princess of Persia by marrying the Persian King Ahasuerus. Esther risks her life to save her people from genocide at the hands of the king's vizier, Haman.

Purim is a morality tale about speaking truth to power. The word *purim* ("lots") refers to the casting of lots by Haman to determine the date upon which he would initiate the genocide of Persia's Jews.

The essential meaning of Purim, as a parable of courage in confronting political evil and injustice, is often lost in its Mardi Gras-like celebration. On Purim, Jews (especially children) dress up as characters from the book of Esther and gather together to read the story of Esther aloud. Whenever the name of Haman is spoken, everyone responds with *graggers* (loud noisemakers), shouts, and the stomping of feet, to remind ourselves to blot out evil from the world.

A second Purim tradition is *mishloach manot*, gifting family and friends with baskets of food and drink. The food most associated with Purim is *hamantaschen*

("Haman's pockets"), a triangular cookie typically filled with poppy seeds, dates, apricots, chocolate, or other sweets. Hamantaschen refers to the pockets of money Haman used to bribe King Ahasuerus into supporting Haman's planned extermination of Persian Jews. In Hebrew, *tash* means "to weaken"; the eating of hamantaschen is a reminder to weaken the power of despots whenever and wherever they arise.

*

PESACH

Pesach (Passover) celebrates the exodus of the Jews from Egypt. It poses two questions for you to consider: To what am I enslaved? and How am I contributing to the sourness of my life and the lives of others?

The word Egypt—mitzrayim in Hebrew—is a Hebrew pun. Mitzrayim means "from the narrow places," and it refers not only to ancient Egypt, but to *tzar'im*, the "narrow places" of enslavement. These can be physical, emotional, intellectual, or spiritual. Pesach is a weeklong exodus from the addictive ideas and behaviors that can enslave each of us.

At the heart of Pesach is the commandment to cleanse your house of leaven and to only consume unleavened foods for seven days (Exodus 12:14, 17). In biblical times, the leavening in bread was always sourdough. Avoiding leaven is a call to put aside the sourness in your house and your life. Every time you substitute unleavened food for leavened food during Pesach, you remind yourself to identify and avoid the sourness that can enslave you, and through which you may enslave others.

The ritual of Pesach revolves around a Seder meal. This includes reading the *Haggadah* ("The Story"), which tells the story of the Jews' exodus from Egypt, and eating foods associated with that story. *Seder* means "order," and speaks to the formal nature of this ritual meal.

One of the most powerful moments of the Seder is the pouring of wine from our glasses while reciting aloud each of the ten plagues suffered by the Egyptians. In this way, we remind ourselves to take no joy in the suffering of others, even if that suffering may be connected to our own liberation.

Another central feature of the Seder is the asking of Four Questions. Traditionally, these questions focus on the customs of this holy day, but I use questions that focus instead on its meaning:

> What can we do to make this night a catalyst for living differently than we do on all other nights?
>
> How does worshipping a god who terrorizes the Egyptians pervert our capacity for compassion?
>
> Would we, like Moses, lack the moral courage to stand against god as Abraham did regarding Sodom (Genesis 18:25)?
>
> How does our imagined innocence—then and now—keep us from taking responsibility for tribalism?

*

SHAVUOT

Seven weeks (s*havuot* in Hebrew) after Pesach, we Jews celebrate Shavuot, which marks the anniversary of the giving of the Ten Commandments on Mount Sinai. (As we will see in Chapter 13, the Hebrew *Aseret ha-Dibrot*, while typically translated as "the Ten Commandments," actually translates as "the Ten Sayings.") Shavuot poses this question to each of us: How free are you?

Central to the observance of Shavuot is the practice of *Tikkun Layl Shavuot*—staying up all night turning Torah, especially the Ten Commandments or Sayings, in light of this penetrating question.

The contemporary French theologian Jean-Yves Leloup (born 1950) asks this question in the following ways, based on the Ten Commandments (or Ten Sayings):

> You are free to live without enslavement and addiction. How free are you?
>
> You are free to live without isms and ideologies. How free are you?
>
> You are free to think rationally, logically, critically. How free are you?
>
> You are free to live without ceaseless toil. How free are you?
>
> You are free to respect and honor your parents. How free are you?
>
> You are free to settle disputes amicably, and without violence. How free are you?
>
> You are free to engage in sex honorably. How free are you?
>
> You are free to live without theft of property or reputation. How free are you?
>
> You are free to live without distorting truth or speaking lies. How free are you?
>
> You are free to live without craving: without judging your success against the success of others, without mindlessly desiring what others have, or what society insists you must have. How free are you?

*

SHMITA AND YOVEL

So far, we have looked at holy days that are celebrated once each year. But Judaism also has entire years of reckoning and reconciliation: *Shmita* (the Sabbatical Year) and *Yovel* (the Jubilee Year).

In ancient times, Shmita and Yovel were practiced by the entire Jewish community. Many of these Jews were farmers or gardeners; some had slaves or indentured servants working for them.

Shmita means "to release." The word refers to allowing the earth to sit fallow during the seventh year of each seven-year cycle (Leviticus. 25:2–7; Exodus 23:10, 11, 12; Leviticus. 26:34, 35). Produce that grows during this period is called *hefker* (ownerless) and may be picked and kept by anyone.

Today, you can still apply Shmita to your life, but not so literally. You can consider every seventh year of your life (ages fourteen, twenty-one, twenty-eight, etc.) a time for deeper questioning. Throughout this year, you can ask yourself: What needs to change in my life to make my efforts at teshuvah and tikkun more fruitful? What do I need to do differently in order to be a blessing to all the families of the earth? The older you become, the richer this time of Shmita can become.

*

In ancient times, after seven cycles of seven years, Jews arrived at the fiftieth year, Yovel, the Year of Jubilee. This was a year of cultural liberation, when all debts were forgiven and all slaves and indentured servants were freed. If, during those fifty years, a family's ancestral land had to be sold in order for the family to survive, that land was returned to the family. Every two generations, everyone had the opportunity to start out fresh. (Some people believe that Yovel historically occurred every forty-nine years—as every seventh Shmita—rather than every fifty. We don't know which of the two is historically accurate, so take your pick.)

Just as Shmita can become a year of self-reflection, so Yuval can be applied to your life as a year of great renewal, reimagining, and transformation.

We all have emotional and spiritual debts to our parents, siblings, and friends. But these debts are not permanent. As you enter your own forty-ninth (or ninety-eighth) year—your year of Shmita—take time for contemplation and self-inquiry. Sit fallow for a time and imagine who you wish to become in your fiftieth (or ninety-ninth) year—your year of Jubilee.

And when that year arrives, stop imagining it and start living it.

*

Many years ago, I was presenting at a Jewish educators' conference. As I sat alone at lunch, a conference participant asked if it would be all right if she joined me and asked for some advice. I agreed, and when she returned with her food, she told me her story.

Her parents were Holocaust survivors whose families were murdered by the Nazis and their collaborators. When she was born, her parents were convinced that she was the reincarnation of her father's sister, who had died in a concentration camp. Her parents raised her to be her dad's sister. She was taught to like what her deceased aunt liked, to imitate the mannerisms of her aunt, and to be what her dad so desperately needed her to be: his sister.

Knowing nothing different, she went along with this for her entire life. Except now something was changing. She couldn't do it anymore. She was angry and rebellious and desperate to be herself, though she was not sure who that self really was. Her question was this: Did she have the right to reject the role her parents imposed upon her? Or, out of loyalty to them and the six million Jews slaughtered in the Holocaust, was she obligated to be a reincarnation of her aunt?

The story was horrifying and her question existential. I had no idea what to say and asked instead how old she was. She was just turning forty-nine. With that bit of information in hand, I knew what to say.

I explained to her about Yovel in the context of the individual rather than the community. I suggested that it was right for her to do what she did for the first forty-nine years of her life, but that any debt she owed to her parents and her people was now paid in full. She should devote her forty-ninth year to self-discovery, so that she might begin to live the second half of her life as she wished, and not as her parents willed.

Had I simply shared this idea as my opinion, it may or may not have carried much weight. But by my linking it to Yovel, she intuited the truth of it, just as I did.

CHAPTER 11

JOY AND GRIEF

As we've seen, haggim, Jewish holy days, are recurring question marks, calling us to regularly assess the quality of our life in the context of being a blessing to all the families of the earth. Jewish life-cycle events, known as simchas (joys), are exclamation points marking important moments of transition along the path of being a blessing. While there are many such moments, we shall consider the four most significant: birth, coming of age, marriage, and death.

*

BIRTH

Birth is an act of divine creativity. As an ocean raises up a new wave, with each birth, God—*YHVH*, the Happening happening as all happening—manifests or incarnates in a new form. While each manifesting is fresh and precious unto itself, all manifestings are the happening of *YHVH*. In the case of human manifestations, each is called to be a blessing to all the families of the earth.

> Every person born into this world represents something new, something that never existed before, something original and unique. "It is the

duty of every person in Israel to know and consider that they are unique in the world in their particular character and there has never been anyone like them in the world, for if there had been someone like them, there would have been no need for them to be in the world. Every single person is a new thing in the world, and is called upon to fulfil their particularity in this world. Every person's foremost task is the actualization of their unique, unprecedented, and never recurring potentialities, and not the repetition of something that another, no matter how great, has already achieved."

(Martin Buber, *The Way of Man*. [London: Vincent Stuart Publishers], 16.)

Realizing your true nature as an incarnation of *YHVH* (Genesis 1:26 speaks of this as tzelem Elohim, the image of God) and cultivating your capacity to be a blessing to all the families of the earth (Genesis 12:3) is what life is all about. Aligning the newborn with this mission is the deeper meaning of the first Jewish life-cycle event: brit/covenant.

A covenant is an agreement between parties. Clearly a newborn child cannot enter into any agreement, so the purpose of brit is to remind the community of their covenant to be a blessing and their obligation to raise the newborn in such a way as to bring them into that covenant.

I offer the following reading, to be read by the parents of a newborn, as one way of affirming their commitment to the covenant and to raising their child within it:

We are humbled by the awesome power of this moment.

The mystery of beginnings is with us, and we acknowledge its presence.

We know neither our destiny nor the destiny of this child.

What we do know is that this life, and all life, is a unique and precious manifesting of Aliveness, called into this world in service to this world.

We vow to raise our child to serve and protect nature (Genesis 2:15); to love neighbor and stranger (Leviticus 19:18; 34); to be a blessing to all the families of the earth (Genesis 12:3) and to share the insights and practices of Judaism to these ends. Blessed is the Source of Life, the Fountain of Being, Whose power enlivens us, sustains us, and enables us to reach this moment of joy.

*

Most people who think of brit most likely think of *brit milah,* the ceremony of male circumcision on the eighth day of a Jewish boy's life. Circumcision is often seen as a primitive act associated with male privilege. In many cases, that is quite accurate. But in the context of Judaism without tribalism, it is an act of resistance to phallic power and patriarchy.

A phallus is a stylized image of an erect penis that represents male power, domination, patriarchy, and all too often, violence. A penis is a potential phallus. Circumcising the penis is an act designed to prevent the penis from becoming a phallus, thereby elevating the male Jew to a position of privilege and power.

Circumcision in the context of Judaism without tribalism is about shifting the ideal of masculinity from one based on power to one based on the Jewish ideals of learning, scholarship, compassion, and a quest for justice. These ideals are—again, in the context of Judaism without tribalism—shared by boys and girls, men and women.

Torah tells two stories of human origins: the first based on dominance and power over nature, the second rooted in service to nature. In the first story, people are created without any connection to the earth and are tasked with ruling over the fish of the sea, the birds of the sky, cattle, nature, and everything that creeps upon the earth. Then they are called to reproduce in such numbers as to subdue nature and have control over the natural world (Genesis 1:26–28).

In the second story, humanity (*adam* in Hebrew) is drawn up from the earth (*adamah*) (Genesis 2:7) and tasked with protecting and serving the natural world (Genesis 2:15). The second story is the story affirmed by Judaism without tribalism. Recognizing the tendency of males to prefer dominating and controlling to serving and protecting, the ceremony of brit milah seeks to promote the latter and prevent the former—all in service to the maturing of a Jewish man whose penis does not empower the worship of the phallic.

Here are the traits of the ideal male in the stories of Genesis: Adam, the mythical first man, was created to be a gardener (Genesis 2:15), and later becomes a farmer (Genesis 3:17). Cain, also a farmer, kills his brother Abel, a shepherd, in what is likely a mythic portrayal of the conflict between farmers (who seek to set boundaries on their land) and shepherds (who prefer a boundary-free world where their sheep can graze freely). As a result of this first murder, Cain ceases to be a farmer and becomes a warlord and founder of a city, an even more boundaried space often demanding protection through violence (Genesis 4:17). While Abel doesn't fare well in this story, the rabbis saw in him the superior man: "Be one of the persecuted and not one of the persecutors; one of the insulted and not one of the insulters" (Talmud, Bava Kamma 93a).

In the story of Jacob and Esau, Esau was a "skilled hunter who preferred the open country," while his twin brother Jacob "preferred to stay at home among the tents." Isaac, their father, loved Esau. Rebekah, their mother, loved Jacob (Genesis 25:27–28). Esau hunted game; Jacob cooked lentil soup (Genesis 25:29).

While the custom of that time saw Esau as the rightful heir to Isaac's tribal leadership, Torah tells a story of reversal, in which the lineage of the Jews derives from Jacob the chef rather than Esau the hunter. As the story concludes, Jacob rejects the warrior life of his brother Esau, preferring instead to tend to the welfare of young children and their mothers, both human and animal (Genesis 33:13).

The purpose of brit milah is to elevate the ideals of gardening, farming, and shepherding—each of which requires respect for and protection of the earth and nature—over the phallic ideals of domination, hunting, and warring.

With this in mind, one of the prayers offered during brit milah is the following:

> May the Source of Life, the Fountain of Being, bestow rest, healing, and full blessing upon this family. May the Ineffable Mystery of Life fill them with good health, strength of body and character, happiness, peace, and length of days. May this child come to know himself and all selves as unique manifestings of the Divine, and may he come to love the world and work for the healing of all creation. May he overflow with wisdom, and walk the path of righteousness, truth, humility, and understanding, honoring both self and other, and being a blessing to all the families of the earth. Amen.

*

PIDYON

Thirty days after the birth of a child, Jewish families engage in the ceremony of *pidyon*, redemption. Until recently, since so many children died during their first month of life, this ceremony marked a child's true embarkation into life.

Many centuries ago, pidyon was linked to the biblical command that first-born male children were to be given to the priesthood and raised to be servants of god (Exodus 22:28–29). In Judaism without tribalism, however, pidyon takes on a psychological twist, redeeming children from the biases and expectations of their parents.

Here is a section of one contemporary pidyon liturgy read by parents:

> Our greatest joy is walking in tune with the universe, in touch with chiut—Aliveness in its myriad patterns and powers. Yet to walk to the rhythm of life, we must be free to walk at our own pace in our own way. We acknowledge this need with this ceremony of redemption.
>
> In ancient times, we consecrated our firstborn sons to priesthood, to choir, and to Temple service. Today we consecrate all our children to life, wisdom, passion, and peace.
>
> May our child find awe, wonder, and wisdom in "the design of the universe, the forces of nature, the nature of time, the orbits of suns and stars, the changing of the seasons, the cycles of years, the minds of animals both domesticated and wild, the power of the wind, the workings of the human mind, the medicinal powers of plants and roots" (Wisdom of Solomon 7:17–22). May our child

see the value of human striving and the worth of human travail. May our child find health and happiness, wisdom and joy, in the world around and within. We hope for the welfare of our child and celebrate the unfolding of this new life venture.

One of the most engaging aspects of Pidyon is the actual ceremony of redemption, in which the rabbi holds the baby in one arm and five silver dollars, provided by the parent(s), in the opposite hand. The baby represents a life unbounded: a unique and unrepeatable manifesting of God who is to be nurtured in service to teshuvah and tikkun. The five coins represent something the parents can control and use as they see fit. Holding baby and coins, the rabbi offers the parents a choice: "Which will you choose: this life whose destiny is unfixed, and who calls to you for guidance through life's uncertainties and insecurities—or these coins, whose value is fixed and whose destiny is yours to control? To which life will you commit your child: to a life of teshuvah and tikkun, returning to God as one's true nature and being a blessing to all the families of the earth—or to a life of domination and control, where money and power are valued over justice and compassion?"

Ideally the parent(s) take the child from the rabbi, who then hands them the silver dollars, to be used to start a college fund. The rabbi then says:

> May you never regret this moment, when you choose to redeem your child from the quest for power and control, preferring instead the awesome path of justice and compassion. It is our fervent hope that you all will live a long and healthy life full of learning, passion, and joy.

*

COMING OF AGE

Coming of age in Judaism happens for girls at the age of twelve and a half, and for boys at the age of thirteen. This is the age when Jewish girls and boys take personal responsibility for the work of teshuvah and tikkun, and for the Jewish mission to be a blessing. This is done in a ceremony of *bat mitzvah* for girls and *bar mitzvah* for boys. Bat and bar mitzvah means "daughter" and "son" of *mitzvot* (the plural of mitzvah)—the commandments through which we Jews live out our mission.

The Hebrew word mitzvah means commandment. A commandment implies a commander—someone outside yourself with the power to demand of you actions that you may or may not wish to perform. In conventional Judaism, this "someone" is the tribal god of the Jews, who chose the Jews from among all humanity to carry out his design for humanity through mitzvot unique to the Jewish tribe. In the context of Judaism without tribalism, however, there is no such commander.

God isn't a being, or even the supreme being, but being Itself. God isn't the creator but creation and creativity. God is *YHVH*, the Happening happening as all happening in, with, and as the entirety of the universe. God doesn't exist; God is existence.

Because this is so, there is no supreme external commander obligating you to perform mitzvot. Instead, Judaism without tribalism recognizes the divine impulse to be a blessing—an impulse that comes from within rather than from without.

With this in mind, the point of becoming a bat or bar mitzvah is to mark a moment in a young person's life when they are free to use the tools of Judaism, in their own way, to achieve teshuvah and tikkun.

At the heart of a bat or bar mitzvah ceremony, the young adult reads from the original Hebrew text of Torah and engages with that text in such a way as to highlight its message—all in service to being a blessing. This demonstrates literacy and literary creativity.

In conventional Judaisms, the reading of Torah is introduced by these Hebrew phrases: *Asher bachar banu mikol ha'amim. V'natan lanu et torato.* These phrases thank god for choosing the Jews from among all the peoples of the earth to receive his one and only revelation: the Torah. This is tribalism at its most explicit.

In Judaism without tribalism, you might use an alternative wording such as this: *Asher bachar banu im kol ha'amim. V'natan kulanu et Torat emet*: "who chose us and all people to receive together teachings of truth."

Part of the ceremony includes the passing of Torah from the parent(s) to the young adult. The parent(s) might recite something like this:

> Sinai calls to you as it called to Moses: establish mitzvot for your life. Torah calls to you as it called to our people: set yourself firmly on the way of teshuvah and tikkun. At this time of maturation, you prepare to ascend the heights of Sinai within. The path is yours alone and you must travel upon it alone. Yet you take with you the love and hope of past years. They will be your companions forever, as we/I will stand ever beside you.

The young adult then takes the Torah, and might say:

> As I have received Torah from your hands, so I accept the challenge of Sinai that comes to me

this day. The challenge is one of both freedom and responsibility, calling me to affirm not only the dignity of self, but the dignity of others as well. It is my heritage this day to enter into a covenant with Life, seeking the mitzvot I need in order to return ever and again to my true self as a manifesting of God, and to recommit over and over again to the challenge to repair the world with justice and compassion, and live my life as a blessing to all the families of the earth.

*

MARRIAGE

While marriage is a universal rite of passage, there are five aspects of Jewish wedding ceremonies that are unique to Judaism: the *ketubah* (the marriage contract), the *chuppah* (the wedding canopy), the exchange of rings, the *Sheva Brachot* (the Seven Blessings), and the breaking of a glass.

In medieval times, the ketubah (marriage contract) obligated a Jewish husband to maintain the financial security of his wife in the event of their divorce. Today, the ketubah is a mutual promise to honor, cherish, and respect one another, even if the union ends in divorce. Just as the couple's love grew out of their friendship, so, if the love fades, the friendship should endure.

As a couple prepares to sign their ketubah, they say to one another:

> We are about to enter into a unique covenant, a bond of body, mind, and spirit. We acknowledge the hurts that are to come and pledge to keep our hearts forever open to healing. We welcome the

joys that are to come, and vow to keep our hearts forever open to wonder. We acknowledge the complexities of life alone and together and promise to keep our hearts forever open to forgiveness.

The chuppah (wedding canopy) under which a Jewish wedding ceremony takes place represents the home the couple is about to establish.

The most important thing about the chuppah is that it has no sides. You'll recall that, in ancient times, it was customary for families to keep the sides of their tents down to ward off strangers—but, according to legend (Midrash Rabbah 48:9), Abraham and Sarah kept the sides of their tent open as an invitation to strangers, offering them rest and sustenance inside. The chuppah's lack of sides reminds the couple to allow their love to be a beacon, and their home a place of welcome to friends and strangers alike.

While it is customary today to use a freestanding chuppah, it is far more powerful to use a chuppah that needs to held up by four people. Whether these are family members or friends, the point is the same: while it is the couple that transitions into marriage, it is the larger community that supports them in their efforts.

It is customary in many cultures to have each partner place a wedding ring on the other's wedding ring finger, while saying something like "With this ring I thee wed." The Jewish ceremony is markedly different. Rings are exchanged in two stages. In the first stage, each partner places the other's ring on the other's right pointer finger (called the "heart finger") rather than on the wedding ring finger. As they do, they say aloud that this ring, if it is accepted, is to be a sign of the couple's commitment to one another. While the couple is free to write their own words for this, one text I recommend is this:

> With this ring I choose you to love and confide in,
> to hold on to, and reach out from. With this ring I
> give you my heart.

Once the rings are placed on each other's heart finger, vows are exchanged. Only then does each partner place their own wedding ring on their own ring finger—thus demonstrating to the assembled group that their marriage is a free act between two consenting adults.

After the exchange of rings, the officiant chants seven blessings. These celebrate (among other things) the divine nature of love, the happiness of the beloveds, and the desire that the whole world live as if at a wedding feast. Among these, the seventh blessing is my favorite:

> Soon may we hear in all our homes and all our communities, in every city and throughout all nations, the voice of joy and gladness, the voice of bride and groom (or groom and groom, or bride and bride), the jubilant voices of people feasting with song. Let this day of union be also a day of reunion. Let each of us take up the challenge of companionship that all the world be joined in friendship and love, and all peoples come together in a harmony of differences beneath the great chuppah of peace.

Perhaps the most well-known tradition associated with a Jewish wedding is the breaking of a glass, which brings the ceremony to a close. The glass represents walls that can creep up, separate, and divide even the most ardent lovers. Holding hands and breaking the glass together symbolizes that, as long as the couple holds on to one another, they have the capacity to shatter these walls and renew their love and friendship.

*

DEATH

Just as birth is the manifesting of the Divine in a new form, so death is the return of that form to its source. Where birth is analogous to a wave arising in an ocean, death is analogous to a wave returning to it.

The moment of death is sometimes called the Kiss of God, that intimate moment when wave realizes its oceanic nature. This is a moment of teshuvah, returning to your true nature as a happening of God. While Judaism has little to say about an afterlife, it does provide a number of traditions that you can use to prepare for the moment of dying. Below are a few of them.

Ethical will. An ethical will is a collection of autobiographical stories articulating both your successes and failures at tikkun (repairing the world with justice and compassion) and being a blessing to all the families of the earth. The idea here is to share these with your loved ones in a manner that informs their own struggles and encourages their own efforts to be a blessing.

Viddui. When you become aware that you are dying, you are encouraged to make amends to those you may have hurt. One way to do this is with the *Viddui*, a verbal confession that affirms your complicity in the suffering of others. If you are too weak to recite the Viddui aloud, you can recite it silently, or a loved one can recite the Viddui on your behalf. Here is a version of the Viddui that I find useful:

> I acknowledge that life and death are not in my
> hands. Just as I did not choose to be born, so I do

not choose to die. May it come to pass that I may
be healed, but if death is my fate, then I accept it
with dignity and the loving calm of one who knows
the way of all things.

May my death be honorable, and may my life
be a healing memory for those who know me. May
my loved ones think well of me and may my memory bring them joy.

From all those I may have hurt, I ask forgiveness. Upon all who have hurt me, I bestow
forgiveness.

As a wave returns to the ocean, so I return to
the One from which I came.

Speaking to the dying. As I sat beside my father's death
bed, I was encouraged by several rabbis to pray to god for
his healing. This type of intercessory prayer doesn't work
for me, as it posits a god who can change the nature of
Reality, rather than recognizes and affirms the God who
is Reality.

I created and offered an alternative, which I offer to you
here. I have substituted my dad's name with "Beloved," and
invite you to insert the name of your beloved in its place.

Listen, Beloved, and yield to the truth of what is
happening: Trust my words. Rest in my voice. Be
still and know all is God.

Listen, Beloved: You are not only the smaller
self with its sensing, feeling, thinking, and doing;
you are also the Greater Self beyond all sensing,
feeling, thinking, and doing. You are not only the
name you carry but the Unnamed that carries you.

Listen, Beloved: You are to this world what a
wave is to the ocean that waves it, a precious and

never-to-be-repeated happening of the One happening as all happening.

Listen Beloved: You are a way the One laughs and weeps and loves and suffers. You are a way the One knows itself as the many. You are a way the Whole knows itself as each part. And soon you will be a way the part comes to know itself as the Whole. You are becoming what you have always been, the nondual Aliveness forever birthing and dying.

Listen, Beloved: You have had many experiences in life. Some matched your desires, others did not; some fulfilled your goals, others did not; some upheld your values, others did not. Some brought you great joy, others brought you great suffering. These may arise in your mind as memories, reflections, yearnings, and regrets. Do not cling to what arises, only acknowledge the arising. Say "yes" to what was without excuse or explanation.

Listen, Beloved: As you die, the faces of loved ones may come to you. Welcome each face with "I love you." Do not cling, excuse, or explain. Without clinging, excuse, and explanation there is only love.

Listen, Beloved: As you die, the faces of those you may have hurt may come to you. Welcome each face with "I am sorry." Do not cling, excuse, or explain. Without clinging, excuse, and explanation there is only forgiveness.

Listen, Beloved: As you die, the faces of those who may have hurt you may come to you. Welcome each face with "I forgive you." Do not cling, excuse, or explain. Without clinging, excuse, and explanation there is only peace.

Listen, Beloved: As you die, you may begin to forget, but you will not be forgotten. You may begin to let go, but you will not be abandoned. You may begin to drift, but you will never be set adrift. You are loved. I am here. You are not alone.

Listen, Beloved: Soon you may find yourself without moorings. This is because moorings are of the past, and you are entering the eternal Present. But you can still hear my voice. Attend to my voice. Trust my voice. Let my voice guide you.

Listen, Beloved: You are yielding to the Light. Allow the Light to draw you closer. You may perceive the presence of others; some you know, some you don't. They are here to comfort you, as I am here to comfort you. Acknowledge them. Feel their love and welcome their support, but do not cling to them. They are here to honor your dying, but they have no place in your death. Let them come, let them go.

Listen, Beloved: The closer you get to the Light, the lighter you will feel. You were a being; now you are be/ing itself. You were a mind; now you are consciousness itself. You were happy and sad; now you are only bliss.

Listen, Beloved: My voice may be fading. My love is not. Let me release you with this prayer—

May you be free from fear.

May you be free from compulsion.

May you be blessed with love.

May you be blessed with peace.

You were loved. You are loved. You are love.

Funerals and mourning. Burial is a simple affair, with one's body wrapped in a shroud and placed in a plain pine box.

There are two prayers central to a Jewish funeral. The first is *El Maleh Rachamin*, a prayer for compassion that invites mourners to make peace with their relationship with the deceased. Here is my version:

> May the One happening as All open our hearts to compassion and our eyes to wisdom, that we might glimpse in perfect peace and sadness the way of all things. May the memory of our beloved be for us a blessing; may we never let the light of our love grow dim in our hearts; and may we remember our beloved kindly and with compassion. God is our source and our destiny, our origin and our destination, our beginning and our end. May this death awaken us to this truth: that the bond of love we shared and share is not severed in sorrow. May our beloved rest in peace. Let us say: Amen.

The second central prayer at a Jewish funeral is the Mourner's *Kaddish*, an Aramaic prayer for peace that provides mourners with the opportunity to make peace among themselves, as well as in the world.

I find the traditional wording of Kaddish, the so-called Prayer for the Dead, with its focus on praising the god of the Jews, next to meaningless. When my dad died, I recited Kaddish in the traditional Aramaic out of respect for him and his Judaism. I continue to recite Kaddish in Aramaic on the anniversary of his death for the same reason. I will do the same when my mom dies. For myself, however, I have replaced the traditional English translation of Kaddish with my own:

> May my grief not cloud my knowing that this life was a birth of God, and that this death a return

to God. May my love for my beloved help me remember that mortality doesn't negate the value of love but indeed magnifies and sanctifies it. May my grief not prevent me from offering love, or my sorrow cause me to push it away when offered. May my memory of my beloved help me to reach out to those in need, helping them lay down their burden, or shoulder it more powerfully.

Death is a suffering that is natural to life. Yet so much of what we bear is an unnecessary suffering, arising not from love but from fear, not from living with death but from dying to life. May I learn to accept the necessary suffering. May I learn to put down the unnecessary suffering and let go of the jagged hurts that I have created for myself and others. May I allow my grief to give rise to compassion—compassion for the deceased, compassion for myself, and compassion for others.

May the One who manifests life throughout the universe be the One upon whom I draw to make my life a blessing to all the families of the earth. Amen.

Following the burial, mourners begin a period of mourning at home called *Shiva*. For some the period is three days, for others the traditional seven. However long one stays at home to mourn, the point of Shiva is to sit with your grief and the love that causes it, so that both can be given full expression.

During this time, the deceased's family is supported by friends and neighbors, who provide food and comfort. One of the traditions associated with Shiva is for visitors to refrain from initiating conversation with the mourners. The goal here is to avert the tendency of visitors to "lighten the mood" of the mourner with small talk, shallow encouragement, and empty platitudes. Rather, visitors are to wait for the mourners to initiate conversation and to allow them to set the agenda for what is shared and said. Shiva is marked by burning a *Yahrzeit* (remembrance) candle that lasts for seven days.

At the end of Shiva, mourners enter a thirty-day period called *shloshim* ("thirty"), during which they are free to reengage with their everyday lives at their own pace. At the end of shloshim, mourners are expected to return to their lives and the work of teshuvah and tikkun.

CHAPTER 12

REMINDERS AND REMEMBERING

While Judaism need not be tribal, Jews are a tribe. And, as with most tribes, we have clothing that marks some of us as members of our tribe. Among these are *kippah*, *tzitzit*, *tallit*, and *tefillin*. In addition to these wearable signs, we also have "wearables" for our homes: *mezuzah* and *Shiviti*.

*

KIPPAH

The Hebrew word kippah means "dome" and refers to the small, round head covering traditionally worn by Jewish men, and now worn by Jews of all genders.

According to our ancient rabbis, you cover your head to remind yourself of the presence of god (Talmud, Shabbat 156b). For me, wearing a kippah is a reminder to keep my thoughts focused on my mission to be a blessing. Indeed, it is because of this mission that I ceased to wear a kippah in public.

After many years of wearing a kippah wherever I went, my wife and I were at an outdoor vegan falafel restaurant in Los Angeles, about to take our first bites of lunch. Suddenly we noticed a very elderly woman racing across one of the busiest streets in LA. She looked like a character from Fiddler on the Roof, and she was screaming at us.

We couldn't make out what she was saying until she reached our table, breathless and flushed. "This restaurant," she said urgently, "it's not kosher." My kippah had triggered her attempt to save us from eating *traif* (non-kosher) food. In that attempt, she had put her own life in danger.

All vegan food is inherently kosher. But, as this woman explained to us, this restaurant had not bothered to pay "the kosher police" (my term, not hers) and secure a sticker that confirmed the restaurant's kosher status. My wife and I thanked her, and slowly made as if we were starting to leave. Satisfied, the woman walked away.

Once she was out of sight, we returned to our table and ate our lunch. But before the first bite of falafel touched my lips, I removed the kippah from my head. I did not want anybody to die because of a hat.

Today, while I do wear a kippah when I teach or attend synagogue, I have replaced it with a fedora or baseball cap when I go out.

*

TALLIT

A tallit is a prayer shawl marked with tzitzit (fringes) hanging from each corner. The purpose of a tallit is twofold. First, it is to cover you so completely that you can no longer distinguish between the rich and the poor based on their clothing. Second, it is to evoke a sense of safety and comfort, like that evoked when a baby is swaddled in a blanket. Sadly, most prayer shawls are more like scarves than blankets and fail to meet either purpose.

Another value of a tallit is that it allows you to shift your focus from what is around you to what is within you. In this it is like the shell of a tortoise: a place of shelter and safety.

*

TZITZIT

When I was a kid in the 1960s, fringes were cool. This had nothing to do with the tzitzit (fringes) on the corners of my tallit (prayer shawl), and everything to do with the TV show *Daniel Boone*. Fess Parker, who starred as Daniel Boone, wore a fringed leather jacket. As a result, so did many American teenagers.

Three thousand years before Daniel Boone, Jews were commanded by god to wear tzitzit on the corners of their tunics (Numbers 15:38; Deuteronomy 22:12). We don't know why, but perhaps it was simply a convenient way of distinguishing Jews' clothes from gentile clothes when they were sold in ancient bazaars.

Tzitzit are fringes tied to the four corners of your clothes, assuming you wear clothes with corners. I don't, so for me tzitzit are the fringes tied to the four corners of my tallit (prayer shawl).

Some Jews compensate for changes in fashion that moved away from clothes with corners by wearing under their clothes a *tallit katan*—a small, four-cornered, poncho-like t-shirt with tzitzit.

Tzitzit are a tool for remembering that God is everywhere and everything. They function as such because of the number of threads and knots needed to make them. Each set of fringes is made of four threads, doubled over to make eight fringes. These threads are then tied with five knots. Adding the numbers 8 and 5 together yields 13.

According to gematria, Hebrew numerology, the three letters of the Hebrew word *echad* (oneness) equal the number 13: alef/1 + chet/8 + dalet/4. Wearing tzitzit on your clothes or prayer shawl reminds you of the oneness of *YHVH* happening as all happening.

While I am not drawn to tallit katan, I am drawn to the meaning of tzitzit and find value in wearing them when wrapped in my tallit during meditation.

*

TEFILLIN

I grew up in an Orthodox Jewish home where my *zayde* (grandfather) and father wore tefillin (phylacteries) during the weekday morning services at our synagogue. While I do not use tefillin daily, on those occasions when I do wear them, I find them powerful tools for reminding myself of my true nature as a manifesting of God.

Tefillin are leather boxes worn during weekday morning prayers. They are secured with leather straps on your arm, hand, and head. If you are not used to wearing tefillin or seeing them worn, they will look very odd at first. But so did a Segway when you saw one for the first time. And while the Segway is not usually the best way to get from here to there, tefillin are an effective way to "be here now."

Inside each small leather box is a Torah text affirming the nonduality of God and calling you to love God by loving all life as manifestations of God (Deuteronomy 6:4–9 and 11:13–21). One box is placed between your eyes, on what other traditions speak of as the third eye. The purpose is to stimulate the shift from mochin d'katnut, narrow mind, to mochin d'gadlut, spacious mind—from self to Self. The second box is placed on your arm, close to your heart. The purpose is to stimulate the shift from selfishness to selflessness, from being a blessing to only those closest to you to being a blessing to all the families of the earth.

Once the second box is affixed to your upper arm, the rest of the strap is wound around your forearm, and then your hand. There are seven windings around the forearm, and the winding around your hand roughly approximates the Hebrew letter *shin*, which stands for power. The number seven represents the seven days of the week. The letter shin reminds you to bind your hand in service to being a blessing. Together, all of this reminds you to be a blessing every day of the week.

Binding your head, heart, and hand with tefillin calls you to unite your thoughts, feelings, and actions in service to teshuvah and tikkun. While most Jews, myself included, no longer use tefillin daily (or ever), having them around where you can see them is often enough to remind you of your true nature and true mission.

Some Jews who are uncomfortable wearing leather tefillin have begun creating vegan tefillin—sometimes jokingly called tofullin. Whatever your tefillin are made from, their point is the same: unite your thoughts, feelings, and action in service to being a blessing.

*

MEZUZOT

The same texts from Torah found in tefillin are found in *mezuzot* ("doorposts"; the singular form is mezuzah). These are small decorative boxes placed on the doorframes of your home, both inside and out. Mezuzot remind you to imbue the activities taking place in your home with justice and compassion.

Traditionally, mezuzot are placed on the doorframes of the rooms in which you live. So, you wouldn't normally put mezuzot on doorframes of closets, pantries, and cellars. Bathrooms are a judgment call.

I have mezuzot throughout my house to remind me to be a blessing. When I enter the kitchen and see the mezuzah, I am reminded that preparing food is a holy activity, often requiring the taking of life. The mezuzah encourages me to cook and eat mindfully and with love. When I enter the living room and see the mezuzah, I am reminded to keep my conversations honest and kind. When I enter the bedroom and see the mezuzah, I am reminded of the holiness of intimacy.

My four-year-old grandson touches mezuzot when he sees them. My son touches them and then kisses his fingers. For me, seeing them is enough to remind me of their message.

*

SHIVITI

Shiviti is the first word of Psalm 16:8: "I place *YHVH* before me always." The word speaks to the Jewish understanding that wherever you turn and whatever you see, you turn toward and see *YHVH*, the Happening happening as all happening.

A Shiviti is a meditative tool—a visual image of the name of God, *YHVH*, and a representation of the menorah, the seven-branch oil lamp featured in the ancient Temple in Jerusalem. Meditating on the Shiviti helps you realize the truth that all life is a manifesting of divine Aliveness, as expressed in this poem by the eighteenth-century rabbi Levi Yitzckok of Berditchev (1740–1809):

You!
Wherever I go: You!
Wherever I stand: You!
Just You. Again You. Always You!
You! You! You!
When life goes well: You!
When life goes poorly: You!
Just You. Again You. Always You!
You! You! You!
Heaven: You!
Earth: You!
Up: You!
Down: You!
Where I turn at every end: You!
Just You. Again You. Always You!
You! You! You!

A Shiviti can come in either a traditional or contemporary form, depending on the artist who creates it.

CHAPTER 13

THE WAY WE WALK

In Genesis 12:1, Abram and Sarai (soon to be renamed
Abraham and Sarah) are commanded to *lech l'cha*, which
is usually translated as "Go forth!" They are to leave their
country, kin, culture, and their parents' home and go to
a place god will reveal to them. The purpose of this journey is to become a blessing to all the families of the earth
(Genesis 12:3).

While the story makes this an outward journey, the
Hebrew phrase lech lecha itself makes it an inner journey
as well: *lech* (walk) *l'cha* (toward your Self).

Commentators on lech l'cha support this interpre-
tation by noting that if this were only an outer journey,
Abram and Sarai would have been told to leave their parents' home first; then take leave of their kin and culture;
and then cross the border of their country and take leave
of that as well. The fact that Torah reverses this order is
a hint (remez) suggesting that the journey is both inward
and outward.

As each of us seeks to be a blessing to all the families
of the earth, we must free ourselves from the constricting
narratives of nationality, ethnicity, culture, race, gender,
religion, and parental bias. If we are to settle in a place
where being a blessing is possible, we must take leave of
those psychological and geographical places where being
a blessing is not possible.

*

If Judaism without tribalism is a walk toward Self and being a blessing (teshuvah and tikkun), *halacha* (also from the word *halach*, "to walk") is the way Jews walk this walk.

According to the third-century CE sage Rabbi Simlai, Judaism is made up of six hundred and thirteen mitzvot, the specific elements of halacha (Talmud Makkot 23b). Rabbi Simlai probably pulled that particular number out of his turban. Also, many of these six hundred and thirteen mitzvot of Judaism are restricted to the Temple, which was destroyed in 70 CE. Still, hundreds of other mitzvot remain. These are more than enough to drive Jews crazy—which is why most Jews ignore most of them.

As noted earlier, mitzvot are said to be commands coming directly from god—or from god's spokesmen, the ancient rabbis. But we can assume that all mitzvot are of human origin—just like the authority of rabbis.

And we don't have to take them as commands. In Judaism without tribalism, mitzvot are inwardly arising techniques for teshuvah and tikkun. Mitzvot help you return to your true nature as a manifesting of God and repair the world by being a blessing to all the families of the earth.

I find the seven mitzvot below most helpful in this regard:

* *Shabbat*, liberating all beings from mitzrayim, the narrow places of enslavement (Deuteronomy 5:15)
* *kashrut*, elevating manufacturing and consuming to the highest ethical and environmental standards

* *tzedakah*, the just use of money and capital
* *kavvanot*, setting your intention with the Ten Sayings (a.k.a. the Ten Commandments).
* *gemilut chasadim*, practicing compassion through the Thirteen Attributes of Lovingkindness
* *shmirat halashon*, cleansing your speech of gossip, slander, falsehood, and distortion.
* *lishmoah*, listening to the hum of *YHVH* happening as all Reality.

Add these to the previously explored practice of turning Torah in search of justice and compassion, and we have an eightfold path (halacha) of Judaism without tribalism.

*

SHABBAT

Shabbat is a weekly day of liberation: "On Shabbat you free yourself from monetized labors—you, your children, your spouse, your employees, your animals, and even the stranger who dwells within your gates" (Exodus 20:10).

While many Jews forbid any kind of creative activity on Shabbat, seeing such activity as "work," the real work prohibited on the Sabbath is work tied to earning a living. On Shabbat, living isn't earned, but celebrated.

What do we do on Shabbat? We "take delight in *YHVH*" (Isaiah 58:13–14), the Happening happening as all happening. Some of us find delight in formal *tefillah* (prayer) and *limmud* (turning Torah) in the synagogue. Some of us find delight in gathering with family and friends. And others among us find delight in making Shabbat a solitary retreat from the world, so that we might "be still and know *YHVH* as the Happening happening as all happening" (Psalm 46:10).

However you engage with Shabbat, the key is the same: liberate yourself from the enslavement to having (Deuteronomy 5:15) and celebrate being (Exodus 20:11).

Here is one meditation I often use to begin Shabbat:

I take the time today to make this day a sabbath. I set aside the labors that define me and uncover the me that cannot be defined. I find in the mitzvot of Shabbat friends and counselors urging me to wholeness.

May these hours of rest and renewal open my heart to joy and my mind to truth. May all who struggle find rest on this day. May all who suffer find solace on this day. May all who hurt find healing on this day. May all who despair find purpose on this day. May all who hunger find fulfillment on this day. And may I live my life in such a way that this day may fulfill its promise.

Shabbat begins at sundown Friday and is marked with the lighting of at least two candles, each with its own individual wick. These candles represent the diversity of creation.

Shabbat ends at sundown Saturday with a ceremony of *Havdalah* ("distinction"). This ceremony helps us shift from the being of Shabbat to the doing of the work week. Havdalah begins with the lighting of a single candle with multiple wicks. This honors the deeper unity underlying all diversity in, with, and as *YHVH*. It is traditional to hold one's fingers near the Havdalah flame and see the blood in your fingertips as a reminder of chiut, Aliveness, that is you at this moment.

Here is the reading that I use for this practice:

Blessed is the One Whose Being is reflected in our becoming. May we illumine this week with the light of truth, revealing the path to compassion and justice.

As the blessedness of Shabbat departs from my heart and my home, may I open myself to compassion that the coming week be graced with kindness.

May this be a week of knowing: knowing truth, knowing love, knowing friendship, and knowing the One who manifests all things and their opposite.

May my labors hasten the perfection of the world, and my kindness awaken those deadened by despair.

May this week arrive for gentleness, good fortune, blessing, success, good health, prosperity, justice, and peace. May it be a week for uplifting the children and honoring the aged. May it be a week of constructive purpose for me, for Israel, and for all who dwell upon this good earth. Amen.

*

KASHRUT

Kashrut (kosher) means "fit." The word speaks to the challenge of maintaining the highest ethical and environmental standards you can muster with regard to all your consuming. A behavior is kosher if it serves our mission of teshuvah and tikkun. A behavior is *treif* ("unfit") if it works against our mission.

While all beings consume to live, humans may be the only animal that lives to consume. We humans sometimes find meaning and purpose in having things. But because that meaning is fleeting (if not downright illusory), we are driven to acquire ever more new and improved things. This chasing and acquiring only perpetuates the idea that we are what we own.

Kashrut doesn't free you from the drive to have—but it moderates it in a way that keeps you from consuming at the expense of being a blessing.

This is most obvious when it comes to food.

According to Torah, the original and ideal human diet is vegan: "I give you every seed-bearing plant that is upon the earth and every fruit–bearing tree—these shall be your food" (Genesis 1:29; 2:16). The medieval Jewish philosopher Joseph Albo (1380–1444) taught that not eating animal flesh would curb our human propensity for violence. If we don't take the life of animals, Albo advised us, we will be less inclined to take the life of a fellow human.

In the story of Noah, the human diet changes after the Flood, when the earth is too saturated to farm, and Noah and his family are allowed to eat the very animals they labored so hard to save. At this point, the relationship between humans and other creatures sours. At that point, "the fear and dread of you humans falls on every animal that walks on the earth, every bird of the air, every creature that crawls on the ground, and all the fish of the sea" (Genesis 9:2).

Kosher is, in a way, an attempt to calm the fears of other creatures by curbing our craving for meat and moving back to the vegan diet of our early biblical ancestors.

The first curb on meat eating comes just two verses after it is permitted: "you may not eat meat with its lifeblood still in it" (Genesis 9:2). Draining an animal of its blood before cooking it is arduous and time consuming. Also, as you probably know from experience, very well-cooked meat usually offers us much less taste and pleasure.

Later, the Torah extends the mitzvah of kashrut by prohibiting cooking a calf in its mother's milk (Exodus 34:26). Many Jews see in this a prohibition against eating meat and dairy together. This further complicates the eating of meat.

Adding to the Jewish carnivore's dilemma is the rabbinic ruling that animals are fit for human consumption only if they are raised for this end and slaughtered in a manner that (at least given the tools available in ancient times) was thought to minimize their pain and suffering (Deuteronomy 12:21). Kashrut prohibits consuming animals that died a natural death in the wild, that were struck and killed on a road (Deuteronomy 14:21), or that were killed through hunting. According to Rabbi Moses ben Nachman (1194–1270), hunting is prohibited to Jews because animals are sentient beings who recognize danger and seek to preserve their own lives. As such, they are not to be killed for either sport or food.

Torah's opinion on eating meat is made clear in the story of manna. After their exodus from Egypt, the ancient Israelites subsisted for a time on manna, a white, sweet-tasting carbohydrate that appeared, like dew, on the earth. But they also complained and demanded meat.

Fulfilling the adage "Beware of what you ask for," god then gave the people meat: "and not for one day only shall you have meat, nor for two days or five days or ten days or twenty days, but for an entire month you shall eat nothing but meat. You will eat meat until it comes out of your nose and you vomit" (Numbers 11:19–20). So much meat was consumed that a plague broke out and decimated the people. The place of their eating and dying was called "The Graves of Lust" (Numbers 11:34).

Concern for the welfare of animals is strong in Judaism, and it is a major part of keeping kosher. This doesn't just involve what you eat. If you see a pack animal suffering under a weight too great for it to carry, you are obligated to alleviate the animal's suffering (Exodus 23:4–5). You are forbidden to muzzle an ox trampling grain on the threshing floor; instead, you must allow the ox to eat some of the grain it is trampling (Deuteronomy 25:4). You are forbidden to yoke an ox and a donkey to the same plow, as their unequal strength will cause them needless strain (Deuteronomy 22:10). All of this is in service to being a blessing to all the families of the earth, including animal families.

When Torah instructs the Israelites how they are to live in the promised land, she again promotes a meatless diet (Deuteronomy 20:19–20). And when they are in exile and dream of returning, they dream once again of a vegan diet (Amos 9:14–15).

Of course, all this was an unrealized ideal. For many centuries, the mitzvah of kashrut continued to function as a way of making meat eating difficult and rare, but not impossible or forbidden.

While I consider kashrut to be part of a Judaism without tribalism, you don't need to follow kashrut as defined and prescribed by ancient (or modern) rabbis. Indeed, Judaism without tribalism encourages you to find your own way to it and into it. Your goal isn't to keep kosher for its own sake, but to keep kosher as a practical expression of being a blessing to all the families of the earth.

Two principles at the heart of kashrut are essential to being this blessing: *bal taschit* (avoiding needless or wanton destruction) and *tzaar ba'alei chayyim* (not causing animals needless suffering or abuse).

Rabbi Moses Maimonides (1138-1204), commenting on Torah's prohibition against destroying fruit trees in a time of war, writes, "Wanton destruction refers not only to the destruction of trees, but breaking vessels, tearing clothing, toppling structures, damming fountains and wells, and causing food to spoil" (Sefer Ha–Mitzvot, Positive Commandment #6). In essence, kashrut requires you to life as mindfully and as lightly as you can.

As part of tza'ar ba'alei chayyim, our ancestors did their best to minimize the physical and psychological suffering of the animals they consumed. Minimizing physical pain requires kosher slaughterers to test their knives for nicks before killing an animal, so as to not cause any extra pain. Reducing an animal's emotional suffering led to a prohibition against taking eggs from a nest when the mother bird is present.

Rabbi Mosheh Feinstein (1895–1986) wrote that "Even though it is permissible [to cause some pain to animals] in order to satisfy human needs by slaughtering animals for food, or by employing animals to plow, to carry burdens or other such things, it is not permissible otherwise to cause them suffering, even when one stands to profit from such practices" (Igg'rot Moshe, Even haEzer 4:92). Referring to the raising of veal calves, he noted that "keeping every calf in its own pen, which is so narrow that it does not have space even to take a few steps ... is certainly forbidden on the basis of tza'ar ba'alei chayyim."

A third pillar essential to kashrut is concern for the welfare of workers. Torah admonishes employers not to cheat their employees or withhold daily wages, even overnight (Deuteronomy 24:14–15).

Many centuries later, Rabbi Judah ben Samuel of Regensburg (1150–1217) ruled that workers must not be burdened by too much work or assigned tasks that they cannot accomplish. Even if a worker asks for more work, the amount given must never exceed a worker's capacity to do it and do it well.

Today, keeping kosher includes honoring workers by promoting safe working conditions, a living wage, paid leave, health care, and other policies that support their well-being.

*

TZEDAKAH

Tzedakah, from the Hebrew word *tzedek* (justice), refers to how you earn and spend your money. According to the Talmud, "tzedakah is equal to all other mitzvot combined" (Talmud, Bava Batra 9b).

So central is justice to Judaism that tzedek is the only word in the entire Torah that is repeated for emphasis: "Tzedek, tzedek, you must pursue" (Deuteronomy 16:20). Indeed, justice is so central to Judaism that it even trumps the morality of god. When god reveals to Abraham his plan to destroy the people of Sodom, Abraham says, "Will you slaughter the innocent with the guilty?.... Such a thing is sacrilege.... Shall the judge of all the world not himself act justly?" (Genesis 18:23–25).

What does it mean that god can commit a sacrilege? It means that god is not the one who establishes what is sacred—people do.

Tzedek, justice, is a human concept. From the point of view of god in this story, might makes right. But Abraham challenges god, insisting that right trumps might.

Abraham then argues for the salvation of the Sodomites. He tells god that god should spare Sodom even if only fifty righteous people live there. God agrees to these terms. Then Abraham argues for forty righteous people, then thirty, then twenty, and then ten. Rabbinic commentators on this story criticized Abraham for not arguing that even the death of one innocent person makes god's act a crime: "to save a single life is to save an entire world" (Talmud, Sanhedrin 37a).

Tzedakah is often confused with charity. But charity, *caritas* in Latin, is an act of the heart that springs from compassion; tzedakah is an act of justice.

Charity appeals to our emotions. That's why so many fundraising commercials on television feature people and animals in heartbreaking conditions. But tzedakah doesn't require you to feel compassion before you reach out to help. Instead, it requires that you look out for the welfare of all beings, regardless of how you feel toward them.

Traditionally, Jews are told to devote ten percent of their annual incomes to promote justice. This might include environmental justice, social justice, racial justice, criminal justice reform, or some combination. How you promote justice is up to you; that you promote justice is not—not if you call yourself a serious Jew.

The most famous set of guidelines for giving tzedakah comes from Maimonides, who offered this nine-point scale for practicing justice through the giving of tzedakah. The items are listed from the most effective to the least:

1) Helping a person start their own business and become self-sufficient.
2) Giving in such a way that both the donor and the recipient remain anonymous.
3) Giving in a manner that only the donor remains anonymous.
4) Giving in a manner that only the recipient remains anonymous.
5) Giving before being asked.
6) Giving after being asked.
7) Giving less than you should but doing so gladly.

8) Giving less than you should and giving grudgingly.

(Maimonides, Mishneh Torah, Laws of Giving to the Poor 10:7-14)

*

GEMILUT HASADIM

Shimon the Righteous, a third-century BCE Jewish sage, used to say, "The world stands on three things: on wisdom, on contemplation, and on acts of kindness (*gemilut hasadim*)" (Pirke Avot 1:2).

Gemilut hasadim differs from tzedakah in this way: "Tzedakah can be given only with one's money; gemilut hasadim can be given with both money and personal service to another. Tzedakah focuses on the poor; gemilut hasadim can be done on anyone's behalf. Tzedakah can be given only to the living; gemilut hasadim can be done for the living and the dead" (Talmud, Sukkot 49b). The most selfless act of gemilut hasadim is caring for the deceased, since only in this case can the donor be certain the recipient will never return the favor (Tanhumah, Va–Yehi 3).

Classic examples of gemilut hasadim include visiting the sick (*bikkur cholim*) and extending hospitality (*hachnasat orchim*). The ancient rabbis told a story of Rabbi Akiva visiting the home of one of his students who had fallen ill. Akiva swept the man's home and cleaned his bedroom. Eventually, the student recovered. When he returned to the academy, the student said to Rabbi Akiva, "You cured me." From that day forward, Akiva taught that one who fails to visit the sick "is like one who sheds another's blood" (Talmud, Nedarim 39b–40a).

Hospitality is central to Judaism. Jewish tradition says

it was a lack of hospitality that caused the Roman destruction of Jerusalem and the exile of the Jews:

A father hosted a wedding feast for his daughter and son-in-law and accidently invited his worst enemy, a man named Bar Kamzeh, instead of his best friend, a man named Kamzeh. Seeing Bar Kamzeh at the feast, the host demanded he leave. Bar Kamzeh offered to pay for half the banquet as long as he was allowed to stay and not suffer the humiliation of being tossed out. The host refused. Bar Kamzeh then offered to pay for the entire banquet, but the host again refused and had him unceremoniously thrown out in full view of all the guests, many of whom were rabbis. Furious that none of the rabbis came to his defense, Bar Kamzeh went to the Roman authorities and denounced the Jews of Jerusalem as plotting against Rome. The city was demolished soon afterward (Talmud, Gittin 55b).

Perhaps the central practice of gemilut hasadim is shaping your life around the Thirteen Attributes of Godliness. These attributes were derived from an ancient rabbinic turning of Exodus 34:6–7. In this story, Moses ascends Mount Sinai to replace the two tablets he had shattered in anger when he saw the Israelites worshipping a golden calf (Exodus 32:19). A thick fog soon surrounds Moses, who hears a revelation on these thirteen attributes of God and Godliness:

1) Seeing oneself as a manifesting of *YHVH*
2) Seeing others as manifestings of *YHVH*
3) Cultivating creativity
4) Cultivating compassion
5) Cultivating grace
6) Cultivating patience
7) Cultivating kindness

8) Cultivating honesty
9) Remembering kindnesses received, rather than nursing grudges
10) Forgiving harm done to you deliberately
11) Forgiving harm done to you accidently
12) Forgiving harm done to you unintentionally
13) Cleansing yourself of delusion

As a human being, you already have these attributes present within you. Your task isn't to implant or absorb these attributes, but to cultivate them.

This is what Torah teaches us when we read that Truth "is not in the sky, for if it were, you would ask, 'Who can ascend to the sky to bring it down to us that we might understand it and live it?' Nor is it across the sea, for if it were, you would ask, 'Who can cross the ocean and bring it back to us that we might understand it and live it?' On the contrary, the Truth is very near to you. In fact, it is already in your mouth that you might speak it, and on your heart that you might live it" (Deuteronomy 30:12-14).

Simply remembering or being aware of the Thirteen Attributes is insufficient. They must be lived.

*

KAVANNOT

Kavannot (the plural of *kavanah*) are affirmations designed to set a specific direction of thought.

Jews have developed hundreds of kavannot over the centuries, but the foundational ones are the ten revealed in the Book of Exodus. The conventional name for these is the Ten Commandments, but this is not their Jewish name. In Hebrew they are called *Aseret ha-Dibrot*, the Ten Sayings.

There is a huge difference between commandments and sayings. Commandments are obligations; sayings are teaching guides. Think of the Aseret ha-Dibrot as a moral compass always pointing toward tikkun.

As sayings, the Aseret ha-Dibrot must be spoken, recited, and affirmed but not necessarily as they come down to us in the fixed text of Torah (Exodus 20: 2-14). Remember, Torah is to be turned creatively so that it does not become fixed and stale. To this end, I have recast the Aseret ha-Dibrot. If my rendering below speaks to you, please use it. If it doesn't, please create your own.

To better understand how I have turned the Ten Sayings, let me remind you of the standard ten:

1) I am the lord your god.
2) You shall have no other gods besides me.
3) You shall not take the name of your lord in vain.
4) Remember the Sabbath.
5) Honor your father and mother.
6) Do not murder.
7) Do not commit adultery.
8) Do not steal.
9) Do not bear false witness.
10) Do not covet.

Here are the Ten Sayings, turned for daily recitation as affirmations of intent:

1) Spiritualty is a source of liberation. Aware of the suffering caused by enslavement to things and ideas, I set my intention to free myself from all addictions and compulsive behaviors, both material and spiritual.

2) God cannot be named. Aware of the suffering caused by gods created in my own image for my own profit, I set my intention to recognize all ideas of god as human notions. These notions are bound by history and circumstance, and forever incapable of defining Reality.

3) God cannot be owned. Aware of the suffering caused by the misuse of god and religion in the quest of power, I vow to liberate myself from all ideologies that demonize others and to honor only those teachings that uphold the freedom and dignity of woman, man, and nature.

4) Remember the Sabbath. Aware of the suffering caused by slavish attachment to work, consumption, and technology, I set my intention to set aside a Sabbath for personal freedom, creativity, and play.

5) Honor the aged. Aware of the suffering caused by old age, I set my intention to care for my parents to the best of my ability and to promote the dignity and well-being of all elderly people.

6) Do not murder. Aware of the suffering caused by violence, I set my intention to cultivate gentleness in all my actions.

7) Avoid sexual misconduct. Aware of the suffering caused by sexual exploitation, I set my intention to never degrade another through the irresponsible or deceitful use of sexuality.

8) Do not steal. Aware of the suffering caused by injustice, theft, and oppression, I set my intention

to respect the property of others, to promote the just sharing of resources, and to cultivate generosity in myself and my community.

9) Do not lie. Aware of the suffering caused by hurtful speech, I set my intention to speak truthfully and with compassion, and to avoid gossip, slander, and discordant speech.

10) Do not covet. Aware of the suffering caused by endless desire, I set my intention to live simply, to avoid debt, and to own only that which brings me joy.

*

SHMIRAT HA-LASHON

Just as the Thirteen Attributes help repair your heart and the Ten Sayings help repair your thoughts, so *Shmirat Ha-Lashon* (literally, "protecting your tongue"), the way of right speech, helps repair your actions.

We humans are speaking animals. The very first thing Adam does in the Book of Genesis is to name all the animals (Genesis 2:20). Naming is a way in which we humans create intimacy. We name our children, our animal companions, and every aspect of the natural world. The more intimate we are with someone, the more loving our names become.

But naming is also a way in which we create enmity. Names can be labels designed to remove intimacy, erase individuality, and encourage or permit exploitation, oppression, and extermination.

Shmirat Ha–Lashon is linked to a teaching of the Baal Shem Tov, Rabbi Israel ben Eliezer (1698–1760), the founder of the Hasidic movement. According to the Baal Shem, each of us is born with a fixed number of words to speak. Which words you speak is up to you, but the number is fixed at birth. When you have spoken the last of your allotted number of words, you die.

While you needn't take this teaching literally, its implication is profound in that it encourages you to speak only when necessary. Further, since you don't know which word may be your last, it admonishes you to ask yourself before you speak, "Is this something for which I am willing to die?"

This test of mindful speech may be sufficient for you. If you'd like more detailed guidance, consider this nine-step guide to right speech created by Rabbi Yisrael Meir Kagan (1838–1933), known as the Chofetz Chaim, "one who desires life":

1) Do not spread a negative image of someone, even if that image is true.
2) Do not share information that can cause physical, financial, emotional, or spiritual harm.
3) Do not embarrass people, even in jest.
4) Do not pretend that writing, or body language, or innuendo is not speech.
5) Do not speak against a community, race, ethnic group, gender, or age group.
6) Do not gossip, even with those closest to you.
7) Do not repeat gossip, even when what you say is generally known.
8) Do not tell people negative things others say about them, for this can lead to needless conflict.
9) Do not listen to gossip; give everyone the benefit of the doubt.

*

LISHMOAH

The final practice we will explore here is *Lishmoah*, Listening.

In a sense, listening has been part of several practices we've already investigated: listening to the intentions of the Ten Sayings, listening to the affirmations of the Thirteen Attributes, and listening to the quality of your speech. But Lishmoah is different. In those other practices, you listen to content; with Lishmoah, you listen to a sound that is free of content.

This sound is called *kol d'mama daka*: the still, almost imperceptible voice of silence. This is the white noise of YHVH manifesting the universe within you and around you.

This soft hiss or hum is behind all the sounds that your ear detects and your brain labels. This is the vibration of YHVH happening as all happening (Genesis 1:2). Like the Sanskrit sound Aum (or Om), kol d'mama daka is the primal sound of all Reality. Unlike Aum, however, it cannot be verbalized. In this is it like the unpronounceable YHVH and the Tao that cannot be named (Tao te Ching 1:1).

You don't chant this sound; you only attend to it. As you do, narrow mind opens to spacious mind, and tikkun unfolds.

Torah introduces us to the notion of kol d'mama daka in the story of Elijah fleeing his would-be murderers and taking refuge in a mountain cave (I Kings 19). During the night, Elijah hears a voice asking, "Why are you here, Elijah?" Assuming this is the voice of his god, Elijah pours out his story of how he is being hounded by people who wish to silence him because of his love for god. The voice instructs Elijah to step out of the cave—i.e., out of the narrow world of his egoic self, mochin d'katnut.

When Elijah does so, he encounters a rock-shattering

wind. Assuming this wind is god, Elijah peers into the wind, only to discover that *"YHVH* is not in the wind" (I Kings 19:11).

As the wind passes, the earth quakes violently beneath his feet. Elijah peers into the quaking, and again discovers that *"YHVH* is not in the quaking."

When the earth settles, the nearby mountain becomes engulfed in flame. Elijah peers into the flame, only to discover that *"YHVH* is not in the fire."

When the fire ceases, Elijah hears kol d'mama dakah—a thin, fragile sound—and is again asked, "Why are you here, Elijah?" (I Kings 19:11–13).

Even the act of stepping outside his cave of self does not awaken Elijah to Self. Elijah still looks for God inside nature. He does not realize that God *is* nature.

Nor does he realize that the question posed is not being asked of his lesser self, *mochin d'katnut*, but of his greater spacious Self, *mochin d'gadlut*. Failing to grasp the nature of the question, and to whom it was addressed, Elijah simply repeats verbatim what he said the first time the question was asked. Had he understood the question from the perspective of spacious mind, he would have answered it from the perspective of Self, saying, "I am here to be a blessing to all the families of the earth."

There is no method or strategy for hearing kol d'mama dakah. This is because no method or strategy is necessary. It merely involves listening.

When I practice this method of no method, something I do each morning, I sit comfortably, close my eyes, and center myself with a version of the *Sh'ma* (Listen!).

The conventional rendering of the Sh'ma is this: *Sh'ma Yisrael! Adonai Eloheinu, Adonai Echad*: Hear, O Israel! The lord your god, the lord is one.

Since I find both "lord" and "god" irrelevant and

inaccurate, I substitute my preferred words: *HaMakom* and *Chiuteinu*.

HaMakom is an ancient rabbinic euphemism for *YHVH* meaning "the infinite place of all happening." *Chiuteinu*, "our aliveness," is a Hasidic euphemism for the same Reality. So, this is what I recite each morning:

> Sh'ma Yisrael! HaMakom Chiuteinu, HaMakom
> Echad: Listen, God-wrestler, and hear the singular
> Aliveness that is the infinite space of God.

I recite the Sh'ma in Hebrew in sync with my breath: breathing in Sh'ma, breathing out Yisrael, breathing in HaMakom, breathing out Chiuteinu, breathing in HaMakom, and breathing out Echad.

When you know that all Reality is the happening of *YHVH*, you simply listen and let it be. You don't seek to accept, or reject, or embrace, or change anything. You simply listen.

When you do, you will hear something more, something very subtle. You will hear kol d'mama dakah: the soft hum of Reality.

Attending to this soft hum, mochin d'katnut opens to mochin d'gadlut. Narrow mind yields to spacious mind, and you return to your true nature. At least for a moment.

PART FOUR
A MANIFESTO

{ CHAPTER 14 }

JUDAISM WITHOUT TRIBALISM: A MANIFESTO

We have covered a lot of material in this book. Some of it you may already have known. Some of it may have been new to you. Most of it was cast in a universalist rather than tribalist light, to show how these teachings and practices can serve the foundational mission of Judaism without tribalism: teshuvah and tikkun.

While I will take up several other aspects of Judaism in the appendixes that follow, let me summarize what I have covered thus far:

> Judaism without tribalism is about being a beacon of light to the world (Isaiah 49:6).

> Judaism without tribalism is about being a blessing to all the families of the earth (Genesis 12:3).

> Judaism without tribalism is about seeing all people as the image of God (Genesis 1:26–27).

> Judaism without tribalism is about knowing God as *YHVH*, the Happening happening as all happening (Exodus 3:14).

Judaism without tribalism is about living without idols, isms, or ideologies (Exodus 20:2–5).

Judaism without tribalism is about loving creation (Numbers 35:33-–4).

Judaism without tribalism is about loving neighbor and stranger (Leviticus 19:18; 34).

Judaism without tribalism is about human dignity (Micah 4:3–4).

Judaism without tribalism is about doing justly, acting kindly, and walking humbly (Micah 6:8).

Judaism without tribalism is about eating simply, working joyously, and loving freely (Ecclesiastes 2:24; 4:8–12).

Judaism without tribalism is about freeing ourselves from tribalism (Genesis 12:1).

Judaism without tribalism is about embracing wisdom rather than fearing god (Proverbs 3:18).

Judaism without tribalism is about living with ambiguity (Eruvin 13b).

Judaism without tribalism is about argument and doubt (Pirke Avot 5:17).

Judaism without tribalism is about ending injustice (Deuteronomy 16:18–20).

Judaism without tribalism is about mindful speech (*shmirat halashon*).

Judaism without tribalism is about wrestling with God (Genesis 18:23–25).

Judaism without tribalism is about arguing for the sake of truth (*machloket l'Shem Shamayim*).

Judaism without tribalism is about cultivating gratitude (*berachot*, Deuteronomy 10:12).

Judaism without tribalism is about practicing forgiveness (Exodus 34:7).

Judaism without tribalism is about protecting animals (*tzar baalei chayyim*).

Judaism without tribalism is about ethical consumption (kashrut).

Judaism without tribalism is about honoring the Earth (*bal tashchit*).

Judaism without tribalism is about ending oppression (Deuteronomy 5:12–15).

Judaism without tribalism is about universal compassion (Shabbat 31a).

Judaism without tribalism is about universal literacy (Deuteronomy 6:7).

Judaism without tribalism is about moving beyond war (Isaiah 2:4).

Judaism without tribalism is about creativity rather than continuity (Psalm 96:1).

ZIONISM AND THE STATE OF ISRAEL

Zionism is a philosophical and political movement founded in the nineteenth century that affirms the right of Jews to determine their own fate in their own land. The State of Israel is the fulfilment of that affirmation.

I am a Zionist insofar as I support a liberal, democratic, Jewishly creative, and yet politically secular State of Israel based in the rule of law, separation of governmental powers, a free press, a free judiciary, free markets, freedom of assembly, free speech, freedom of and from religion, and the full enfranchisement of all citizens regardless of race, ethnicity, religion, sex, gender, etc. In other words, what I want as a Zionist is essentially an idealized version of the United States of America with a Jewish majority. When the State of Israel strives toward these ideals, I support its efforts. When it doesn't, I don't. I can say the same regarding the United States.

*

According to the *Oxford English Dictionary*, ethno-nationalism is "the advocacy of or support for the political interests of a particular ethnic group, especially its national independence or self–determination." As banal as this sounds in theory, in practice this often means the advocacy of the interests of one ethic group over those of others. In this sense, ethno-nationalism is essentially tribalism.

Just as I support the State of Israel when it resists ethno-nationalism and the degradation of liberal democratic values, I withdraw my support when it morphs into ethno-nationalism and violates liberal democratic ideals. I can say the same regarding the United States.

*

The term Zionism refers to Zion, another name for Jerusalem. In this way, Zionism is a movement to turn the closing cry of the Passover Seder, "Next year, in Jerusalem!", into a reality.

For centuries "Next year in Jerusalem" was a prayer whose fulfillment was left to god. Many Jews expected that god—their god, the god who chose them, gave them Torah and the deed to the promised land—would eventually anoint a messiah (*mashiach* in Hebrew, meaning "the anointed one") as heir to the throne of King David and bring the Jews of the diaspora back to Israel. In the meantime, Jews stayed where they were, doing their best to be good citizens of the countries in which they lived.

This changed in the late 1800s with a rise in Jew-hatred among Europeans and the influence of an essentially godless Jewish identity among secular European Jewish elites. For these Jews, assimilation into European society was their messianic hope—a hope shattered as Jew-hatred increased, especially in countries they thought to be the most liberal and enlightened, such as Germany and France.

Napoleon Bonaparte (1769–1821) enfranchised Jews as individuals in the First French Republic in hopes of assimilating them into his empire. This failed on two fronts: the Jews clung to their Judaism and Europeans clung to their antisemitism.

As Europe became more nationalistic, Europeans became more antisemitic. This led Theodor Herzl (1860–1904), who lived in Hungary and Austria and had no faith in god, to consider Jewish integration into European society a pipe dream. In 1895, Herzl published *The State of the Jews*, in which he claimed that only self-governance would free the Jews and put an end to antisemitism. Two years later he convened the First Zionist Conference in Basel, Switzerland. This conference marked a sea-change in Jewish life: Jews would no longer wait on god to return them to the promised land and reestablish the Jewish state. Instead, they would do this themselves.

*

The goal of Zionism was—and is—to create and maintain a Jewish homeland in Palestine. The establishment of a Jewish homeland would trigger the renewal of Jewish civilization and a renaissance of Jewish language, art, music, literature, religion, etc.

Some early Zionists felt that this homeland required political sovereignty, a Jewish military, and Jewish rule over the Palestinians already living in the land. Others felt that such a homeland could foster a cultural renaissance without political autonomy and military superiority. In other words, Zionists argued over whether the future state was to be a *medinat Yehudit*, a Jewish state, or a *medinat Yehudim*, a state of Jews. In the end, political Zionism won out over cultural Zionism, and the State of Israel became a medinat Yehudit, a Jewish state.

*

While the State of Israel is in many ways democratic, it is also unmistakably ethno-nationalist, privileging Jews over Palestinians. As the Nation-State Law in 2018 puts it: "the right to exercise national self-determination in the State of Israel is unique to the Jewish People." To the extent that this is so is the extent that Israel is not a true democracy, when by democracy we mean a system of government that equally enfranchises all its citizens. While the State of Israel is more democratic than other ethno-nationalist states—Turkey, Hungary, China, Russia, and most Arab and Muslim countries, for example—when push comes to shove, I fear that the ethno-nationalist Jewish character of the state will trump its liberal democratic impulses.

This is not unique to Israel, On the contrary, it is the hallmark of ethno-nationalism. Criticizing Israeli eth-no-nationalism is—for those who, like myself, claim to support liberal democracy—totally justified. Criticizing Israeli ethno-nationalism alone and excusing or ignor-ing the evils of other ethno-nationalisms is unjustified. To stand by your principles is laudable. To cherry-pick where to stand on them is hypocritical. At the very least, those liberals who limit their criticism to Israel alone are hypocritical at best, and antisemitic at worst.

*

While some white Christian Americans wish it were oth-erwise, the United States is not (at least not yet) an eth-no-nationalist Christian state privileging white European Christians and rightwing white evangelical Protestant Christianity.

At least in theory, what makes Americans American isn't religion or ethnicity but a shared allegiance to the sacred principles of liberal democracy, as enshrined in documents such as the Declaration of Independence, the Constitution, and the Bill of Rights. In the United States, again in theory, religion in general—and Judaism in particular—are supposed to be a private affair. In Israel, however, Judaism is a matter of social, cultural, and even political cohesion.

This difference is often a source of much confusion and conflict between Israeli and American Jews, because the privatization of religion is seen by American Jews as key to their survival as Jews in America, whereas the privatization of religion in Israel is seen by Israeli Jews as a threat to the Jewishness of their state. Given the very different natures of these two nations, this confusion and conflict won't go away anytime soon.

*

In 1975, the UN General Assembly passed Resolution 3379, equating Zionism with racism. This was a political act of Jew-hatred. The UN General Assembly itself realized this and repealed the resolution in 1991. The fact that it took the General Assembly sixteen years to do so attests to the systemic hatred of (or at least indifference to) Jews among the world's nations.

While antisemites today continue to claim that Zionism is racist, that claim is blatantly false. Jews are not a race— indeed, Jews comprise all races. But while Zionism is not racist, neither is it intrinsically democratic—or resistant to the allures of ethno-nationalism.

Today, the State of Israel is home to over 1.5 million Palestinian Israeli citizens. It controls almost five million more Palestinians under occupation. Zionism wasn't created to handle this. As a result, Zionism is caught between a rock (an ethno-nationalist form of apartheid) and a hard place (secular democracy and an end to ethno-nationalism). Unless and until Zionism finds a way out of this dilemma, its confused and controversial treatment of Palestinians and other non-Jews will continue to create hardship for millions of human beings. In so doing, it violates the very foundation of Judaism as a vehicle for teshuvah and tikkun— being a blessing to all the families of the earth.

*

The conflict at the heart of contemporary Zionism is the conflict between liberalism and illiberalism, between secular democracy and ethno-nationalism, and between a Judaism without tribalism and a tribalist Judaism. While the conflict plays itself out in the Israel-Palestine conflict, the central battle is in the soul of the Jews.

For millennia, Jews dreamed of a homeland where "justice rolls like water, and righteousness is a never drying river" (Amos 5:24); where justice, compassion, and religious humility replace oppression, cruelty, and religious triumphalism (Micah 6:8); where swords are beaten into plowshares and spears into pruning hooks, and war and the preparation for war are eliminated (Isaiah 2:4); and where all people can sit on their own property without fear of their government or their neighbors (Micah 4:4). What looks so hopeful and inviting in the pages of the Jewish Bible turns out to be a near-impossibility today, given the politics of the Jewish state.

*

The Jewish claim to the land of Israel (also known as Canaan) is rooted in the notion that god gave the Israelites the land in perpetuity. Yet this Jewish claim to the land of Israel is rooted in fantasy. While the god of the Jews privileges the Jews, the God of the universe, *YHVH*, the

Happening happening as all happening, does not. Because tribal gods often show their support by decimating other tribes, it should be no surprise that the god of Israel uses genocide to fulfill his promise to the Israelites: "When Adonai your god brings you into the land you are to conquer, many nations must be defeated: the Hittites, the Girgashites, the Amorites, the Canaanites, the Perizzites, the Hivites, and the Jebusites—seven nations, each larger than and militarily superior to you. And yet Adonai your god shall deliver them to you, and you shall defeat them and completely destroy them. Make no treaty with them. Show them no mercy" (Deuteronomy 7:1–2).

As morally repugnant as this may be, it isn't unique to the god of the Israelites. Christianity and Islam have a no-less violent god. The difference between the god of the Jews and the gods of the Christians and Muslims is that the Jewish god is the invention of ancient Israelite leaders who wanted to occupy Canaan, while the Christian and Muslim gods are the creation of leaders who want to occupy the whole world.

The moral of this story is clear: beware of gods with guns.

*

The Jews have a state of their own because of the geopolitics of the nineteenth and twentieth centuries. They maintain the State of Israel because they have the military might to do so. And they have the military might to do so because the United States secures that might. As long as this remains the case, the State of Israel will exist. This has less to do with god and more to do with guns.

This isn't unique to Israel. If the Tibetans had the means, China would no longer occupy Tibet. If the Syrians had the means, Bashar al-Assad would not still be the president of Syria. And if the Confederate States of America had the means, people living in Massachusetts would need a passport to visit Miami, Florida.

*

The United States' special relationship with the State of Israel rests on at least five factors: 1) about one half of the world's Jews live in the US; 2) they vote; 3) Israel is the only democracy in the Middle East; 4) white Evangelical Christians see in Israel ethno-nationalism what they hope to create in the United States, an ethno-nationalist Christian nation that privileges the rights and values of white Evangelicals; and 5) white Evangelical Christians need the Jews to return to Israel to trigger Armageddon, the final battle between good and evil, and usher in the second coming of the Christian god.

*

Years ago, I was part of a group of Nashville rabbis and evangelical pastors who toured the State of Israel together to foster mutual understanding among us. A highlight of the trip for the pastors was a visit to the hill of Megiddo, where Armageddon is to take place.

As we stood on the hill, the pastors read from the Book of Revelation and explained to us how god would destroy all the unbelievers and that their blood would fill the valley as high as a horse's bridle and for a distance of two hundred miles (Revelation 14:20). Perhaps to make us rabbis feel better about this horror, they also promised that, while millions of Jews would die in this conflict, one hundred and forty-four thousand would survive, convert to Christianity, and recognize Jesus as the true messiah in time to save themselves (Revelation 14:1).

We rabbis were stunned. But we shouldn't have been. Tribal gods love war and revel in the destruction of their enemies: "Now go and attack Amalek, and utterly destroy all that they have; do not spare them, but kill both man and woman, child and infant, ox and sheep, camel and donkey" (I Samuel 15:3); "At the end times the son of man will unleash his angels to rake his kingdom free of sin and evildoers, who will be tossed into a fiery furnace, screaming and grinding their teeth in agony" (Matthew 13:40–42); "And kill the unbeliever wherever you find them" (Qur'an 2.192).

*

Many Jews, especially liberal American Jews, hold out the hope for a two-state solution, in which a thriving Palestinian state lives peacefully side by side a thriving Jewish state. While there may have been a time when this was a possibility, that time is long gone, and maintaining the fantasy of "two states for two peoples" simply allows the status quo to continue.

As long as Israelis and liberal American Jews pretend a Palestinian State is possible, they can pretend that the oppression of the Palestinians in the Occupied Territories is, while morally reprehensible, temporary and hence acceptable. And as long as Palestinians pretend that they can defeat the State of Israel and establish a new state from the Jordan River to the Mediterranean Sea, they can blame Israel for all their suffering and ignore the abuse they receive at the hands of their own leaders, who use god and guns to maintain their own power, while doing nothing to actually establish Palestinian self-rule.

*

Peace will come to Israel/Palestine when Israelis and Palestinians tire of killing for gods who never tire of killing, cease to call their respective dead martyrs, and begin to see themselves for what they are: tragic victims of two violent ethno-nationalist fantasies that happily sacrifice the many for the private benefit of the few.

JEW-HATRED

I prefer the term Jew-hatred to antisemitism. It is more honest. An antisemite is one who hates Jews for no other reason than they are Jews. Hating Jews is not the same as criticizing Jews, and certainly not the same as criticizing individual Jews. Criticism of Jews for this or that behavior or trait becomes Jew-hatred when the criticism is reserved solely for Jews, while excusing others who may exhibit the same behavior or trait.

Similarly, criticizing the State of Israel when its policies violate liberal democratic values is not antisemitic. Criticism of the State of Israel alone, while ignoring or excusing other nations worthy of the same criticism, is antisemitic. Criticism of Zionism when Zionism morphs into ethno-nationalism is not antisemitic. Criticism of Zionist ethno-nationalism alone, while ignoring or excusing other nations worthy of the same criticism, is antisemitic. Being anti-Zionism and anti-Israel and arguing against the Jewish people's right to self-determination and sovereignty is antisemitic, even when done by Jews.

*

In 1998, the International Holocaust Remembrance Alliance created what it called a Working Definition of Antisemitism: "Antisemitism is a certain perception of

Jews, which may be expressed as hatred toward Jews. Rhetorical and physical manifestations of antisemitism are directed toward Jewish or non-Jewish individuals and/or their property, toward Jewish community institutions and religious facilities." While Jews, because we are Jews, argue over the validity of this definition of antisemitism, the truth is that Jew-haters don't much care for definitions.

As I have argued previously, a Jew is anyone who says they are a Jew. For Jew-haters, a Jew is anyone they say is a Jew. This is why there is Jew-hatred in countries that have no people who call themselves Jews. In such countries, "Jew" simply becomes a label someone attaches to their enemies.

*

Jew-haters offer many reasons for their hatred of Jews: Jews are rich, they dominate the media, they control the government, they are capitalists, they are socialists, they are communists, they are Zionists, they are anti-Zionists, they are cosmopolitan, they are ethno-nationalists, they are white, they are people of color. The simple truth is Jew-haters hate Jews for one simple reason: they are Jews.

*

Jew-hatred has its roots in Christianity. In the Gospel of John, Christians are taught that Jews are the children of Satan (John 8:44). The Book of Revelation tells Christians that Jews who reject Jesus belong to the synagogue of Satan (Revelation 2:9; 3:9). This particular charge still holds sway among some people. In fact, that message was literally mailed to many synagogues on January 27,

2020, the seventy-fifth anniversary of the liberation of the Auschwitz-Birkenau death camp.

*

John Chrysostom (347–407), an early Church Father, taught that because Jews rejected Jesus, they should be slaughtered. Chrysostom cites Luke 19:27 as his source for this conviction. In this passage, Jesus says, "as for those who do not want me to rule over them, they are my enemies. Bring them here and murder them before me."

Christian Jew-hatred has only deepened over time. In his book *On the Jews and Their Lies*, Martin Luther (1483–1546) promoted a seven–point program regarding the Jews: 1) burn down their synagogues and schools, 2) demolish their houses, 3) confiscate their holy books, 4) make the teaching of Judaism a crime punishable by death, 5) deprive Jews of safe passage when they travel, 6) confiscate Jewish wealth, and 7) conscript young Jewish men to work on Christian farms—or exile Jews from one's country altogether. And all this was "to be done in honor of our lord and of Christendom, so that god might see that we are Christians...."

The god of John Chrysostom and Luther, like all tribal gods, sanctions violence in service to his own aggrandizement. Indeed, this is how you know if your god is God: if your god calls you to kill or die for him (and gods are almost always male), you can be certain your god isn't God.

*

Next to the New Testament and Luther's *On the Jews and Their Lies*, the most famous antisemitic book is *The*

Protocols of the Elders of Zion. This was a Russian literary hoax based on an 1860 French satire that had nothing to do with Jews or Judaism. *The Protocols* was written by the Russian secret police and published in 1903, for the purpose of stirring up the Russian people against Jews.

The Protocols of the Elders of Zion purports to be the minutes of a secret meeting of Jewish leaders. At this meeting, they discuss their plan for global domination by undermining Christian values and controlling global finance and the press.

Despite the fact that *The Protocols* was proven to be a scam by the *New York Times* in 1921, the book continues to be translated, published, and used to justify Jew-hatred around the globe, especially in the Middle East.

The book's three major lies—that Jews harbor anti-Christian values, that Jews control the world's financial systems, and that Jews control the press—remain the foundation of most Jew-hatred to this day.

*

Hitler didn't invent Jew-hatred; he inherited it and racialized it. For most Christians, Jews were a religious group worthy of disdain and even destruction. But for Hitler, the Jewish religion was beside the point. As early as 1922, Hitler was writing that Jews were a race carrying disease and infecting the Aryan body politic. As such, Jews had to be exterminated, just as one exterminates disease-carrying rats. The disease Jews carried was whatever Hitler didn't like: capitalism, communism, cosmopolitanism, etc.

Nazi Jew-hatred found fertile soil in the hearts and minds of Europeans. It in no way disappeared with the defeat of the Third Reich. In 2018 alone, France's National

Human Rights Advisory Committee reported a 70 percent increase in crimes against French Jews over the
year before. A German government study reported a 20
percent increase in Jew-hatred among Germans. A 2017
study documented that acts of Jew-hatred in the United
States had risen 57 percent. Things have only gotten worse
since then. Crimes are easily measurable; hatred is not.

*

Jew-hatred is often couched as opposition to the State of
Israel. But having strong disagreements with the State of
Israel—or opposing some of its actions, laws, or policies—
is not anti-Israel, anti-Zionist, or antisemitic. However,
being opposed to the very existence of a Jewish homeland
is antisemitic.

The key word is anti. If I am "anti" something, I want
to see that something ended. If I am antislavery, I want
slavery to end. If I am anti-racist, I want racism to end.
If I am anti-misogyny, I want hatred of women to end.
Similarly, if I am anti-Israel, I want Israel to end, and if I
am antisemitic, I want the Jewish people to end. Desiring
the end of Israel is a far cry from criticizing the country's
laws or policies.

The same is true of anti-Zionism. Criticizing Zionism
is not antisemitic. Encouraging more sanity and compassion in Zionism is not antisemitic. But being anti-Zionist is antisemitic. Zionism is the movement to support,
procure, and maintain Jewish autonomy and self-determination in the State of Israel. Anti-Zionism is the effort
to deny the Jewish people—and only the Jewish people—
this autonomy and self-determination.

*

People who call out the State of Israel for its oppressive posture toward Palestinians, and their legitimate quest for autonomy and self-determination in their own state, are not necessarily antisemitic. In fact, many Jews, including many Israeli Jews, feel that, as Jews, they are obligated to speak out against such injustice. But people who call for the dismantling of the State of Israel, while ignoring the injustices done by other ethno-nationalist states such as Russia, China, Turkey, Hungary, Poland, Iran, Syria, Egypt, and Saudi Arabia, are acting out of antisemitism, not out of a sense of justice.

*

As Jews, how can we best respond to antisemitism and combat Jew-hatred?

First, be a proud and engaged Jew. For me, this means 1) devoting yourself to teshuvah and tikkun; 2) affirming cosmopolitanism and a greater human unity beyond nation-states; 3) cultivating a love of words and word-smithing, and a level of critical thinking that shatters the foundation of uncritical believing; 4) strengthening your skepticism regarding authorities of all stripes; 5) celebrating humor as a way to reveal that the emperor—our religious and political leaders—often has no clothes; 6) working to end racism, misogyny, xenophobia, and the like; and 7) promoting liberalism, socially conscious capitalism, and the inalienable rights of individuals to life, liberty, freedom of speech, freedom of assembly, freedom of and from religion, and the pursuit of happiness.

Second, work with other oppressed peoples to protect one another from hate and oppression.

Third, work with other Jewish groups to root out oppression in Jewish life, including the oppression of women, queer folk, Palestinians, etc.

Fourth, live a positive Jewish life rooted in the Jewish mission of teshuvah and tikkun: returning to your true nature as the image of God, and repairing the world with justice and compassion by being a blessing to all the families of the earth.

JESUS

Jesus is arguably the most famous and influential Jew who ever lived. As such, it is an act of tribalist myopia to banish him from the tribe. Jesus was born a Jew, lived as a Jew, and died because he was a Jew. Rejecting Jesus because of the failure of Christians to live out his teachings is like rejecting Gandhi because of Indian Prime Minister Narendra Modi's love of Hindu nationalism. Hence, Jesus's inclusion in this book.

*

I know Jesus as a Jew, and, hence, as my cousin.

I know Jesus as a Wisdom sage, and, hence, as one of my teachers.

I know Jesus as a social prophet and revolutionary, and, hence, as one of my role models.

I know Jesus as a God-intoxicated mystic, and, hence, as one of my rebbes.

I know Jesus as a Self-Realized human, and, hence, as a source of hope.

*

As a Jew, Jesus was called to the mission of the Jew: teshuva and tikkun. He achieved the first when he realized that he and God were one (John 10:30). He achieved the second when he taught "Whatever you do for the least among you, you do to me" (Matthew 25:40).

As a Wisdom sage, Jesus was drawn more to Judaism's teachings of nonduality and compassion than to its laws. When asked to articulate the whole of Torah, Jesus, para-phrasing his teacher Hillel, said, "Whatever you wish others do unto you, do unto them, for this is the entire Torah and the prophets" (Mark 7:12).

As a prophet and revolutionary, Jesus taught that if a Roman soldier strikes you on the right cheek—something Roman occupation law allowed as a sign of Roman supe-riority—dare him to strike your left cheek—something Roman occupation law did not allow, as it signaled equal-ity between two people.

And Jesus taught that if a Roman soldier commandeers you to carry his rucksack for one mile—something also allowed by Roman occupation law as a sign of Roman superiority—you should offer to carry it a second mile—something Roman occupation law did not allow, as it, too, signaled equality between two people.

And Jesus taught that if the corrupt court took your outer garment as payment for your failure to pay a debt, you were to give the court your underwear as well, as a statement of civil disobedience (Matthew 5:38–42).

As a God-intoxicated mystic, Jesus taught, "I am like a vine and you are like my branches. If you remain in me and I in you, you will bear much fruit; but apart from me you can do nothing" (John 15:5).

*

Jesus lived under a brutal Roman occupation that was enforced by terror. He also died because of it. Crucifixion was the preferred method of Roman terror, and thousands of Jews were left to rot on wooden crosses as a warning to the people against committing acts of rebellion against Rome. While Jesus eschewed violence—"Blessed are the peacemakers" (Matthew 5:9); "All who take up the sword are put down by the sword" (Matthew 26:52)—his teaching attracted large crowds, and the Romans were concerned that large gatherings of Jews could be incited to acts of resistance against Rome.

While most Jews who knew Jesus loved him (Matthew 21:1–11; Mark 11:1–11; Luke 19:28–44, and John 12:12–19), some—especially the priestly class, whose power, status, and financial well-being depended on collaboration with Rome—opposed him to maintain the status quo.

*

The Gospels were written decades after the events they portray by men who wanted to create a religion about Jesus rather than, as Jesus did, reform the religion of Jesus—i.e., Judaism. Where Jesus focused most of his efforts on his fellow Jews, the founders of Christianity sought a more global religion. To free their Jesus from his Judaism, they portrayed Jews as being anti-Jesus; demonized Judaism as the synagogue of satan (Revelation 2:9; 3:9); and demonized the Jews as the children of satan (John 8:44).

*

The most damning Gospel story regarding the Jews is the story of Barabbas (Matthew 27:15–26). According to the Gospels, Jews were allowed to select one prisoner to be released by Pontius Pilate each Passover. In the story, the Jews were presented with two prisoners, Jesus and

Barabbas and forced to choose between them. They chose Barabbas.

The story is pure fiction in service to Jew-hatred. Here is how we know: 1) Roman occupation law never allowed for the release of a prisoner at Passover; 2) Barabbas is Aramaic for "son/bar of the father/abbas"; 3) according to an early manuscript of Matthew's Gospel, Barabbas's first name was "Jesus"; 4) the chances of Pilate having two prisoners both named Jesus bar Abbas (Jesus Son of the Father) are nil; and 5) the Gospels offer no rationale as to why the Jews who loved and welcomed Jesus into Jerusalem on Sunday would suddenly turn on him the following Friday.

My sense is that the Gospel fiction of Barabbas was a perversion of what actually happened: the Jews who loved Jesus stormed the prison demanding the release of Jesus Bar Abbas. This was an act of civil disobedience that scared both Jewish and Roman leadership into crucifying Jesus in hopes of putting an end to his reformation of Judaism and his threat to Roman occupation.

*

While Jesus was a great sage and spiritual revolutionary, he was not the Jewish messiah. This is because he failed to fulfill the Jewish messianic mission: He didn't free the Jews from Roman oppression. He didn't establish a Jewish state that was a light unto the nations (Isaiah 42:6) and a blessing to all the families of the earth (Genesis 12:3). And he didn't bring an end to war and establish a new world order based on compassion, justice, and humility (Micah 4:3; 6:8).

While many Christians believe that accepting Jesus as your personal messiah will bring you eternal life in a future world—"For god so loved the world that he gave his only begotten son that whoever believes in him shall not die but gain eternal life" (John 3:16)—Jews are unconcerned with eternal life. This is not our concern regarding the idea of a messiah. We want a messiah who will bring collective peace to all creatures in this life.

*

For centuries, Christians have sought to convert Jews to Christianity—sometimes under threat of death or exile. While the threats are gone, the effort continues. Yet very few Jews actually become Christians. The reason for this is simple: Christianity solves a problem Jews don't have.

"Baptism, by imparting the life of Christ's grace, erases original sin" (Catechism of the Catholic Church, 405). That's great if original sin is your problem. Jews, however, never heard of it. The Jewish problem is exile: a loss of our true nature as a manifesting of *YHVH*. The solution to the Jewish problem is teshuvah and tikkun, not belief in Jesus Christ as our lord and savior.

ADVICE FOR CONGREGATIONAL RABBIS

I was a congregational rabbi for twenty years. Here is what I recommend to congregational rabbis based on my experience.

My guess is that much of what I say below is also relevant to rabbis in noncongregational settings as well as to clergy in general.

*

Numbers matter.
Attendance at worship services and educational programs is how you know whether you're offering something that people want. If the numbers are low, don't survey the congregation to find out what they want. What they want is not to attend. Instead, offer what you want to offer. If no one comes, find another synagogue—or another line of work.

*

Shrink your synagogue.
If your sanctuary is so big that you usually play to a largely empty room, sell the building and move into a facility that reflects your reality.

*

Talk about what matters.
What matters is teshuvah and tikkun. What matters is
how to make sense out of the senseless; how to make
meaning out of the meaningless; and how to navigate the
madness, joy, and tragedy of life. Of course, you never
learned how to do any of this in rabbinical school. The
assumption there was that Judaism matters to Jews—or,
if it doesn't, that you can make it matter. But if it doesn't,
you can't make it matter.

*

Forget answers. Ask questions.
Most people don't come to you to learn what to do. They
come to have you excuse what they are already doing. If
you won't do that, they'll be tempted to find a rabbi who
will. Don't be that rabbi. Instead, be the rabbi who helps
them to question what they are doing and to explore how
they might do it differently.

*

Never eat during congregational meals.
Most people won't bother to make an appointment to talk
with you in your office. Most will grab you during a meal
and expect you to answer the most pressing question in
their world, right then and there. You have to answer, of
course. But doing so with your mouth full of bagel is difficult and unsightly.

*

Always carry a beverage during congregational meals.
Water works as well as coffee. You aren't carrying the cup because you're thirsty; it's a prop. When people ask you to answer their most pressing questions, nod thoughtfully and take a slow sip of whatever it is you are carrying. This will provide you with several seconds to concoct an answer.

✳

Refer.
When congregants come for advice regarding (for example) their collapsing marriage, they don't want to hear how Sarah and Abraham stuck it out for a lifetime, even though Abe pimped out Sarah to the Pharaoh, Sarah tried to murder Hagar and Ishmael, and Abe took it on spec to sacrifice their son Isaac. They don't want to hear anything Jewish at all. They want marriage counseling; they just don't want to pay a marriage counselor to get it. Listen attentively, nod compassionately, and then refer them to a professional.

This goes for every situation in which congregants essentially want counseling. If you aren't licensed to give advice on a topic, keep your opinions to yourself.

✳

Be fire-worthy.
Chances are you're going to be fired. You don't have to do anything to get fired other than grow older. At some point, you will be too old to "relate to the kids." Or too old to bring in younger families. Or so old that your board of directors fears having to pay you as a rabbi emeritus. So, when you're in your fifties, someone on your board is going to find a way to force you out.

Knowing that it's coming, do something in your fifties that is worth getting fired over. Here's what I suggest: tell your congregants the truth that religion is made up; that God doesn't choose one people over another, write books, or dabble in real estate; that making a fetish out of the Holocaust and Israel isn't a substitute for living Jewishly.

*

Israel isn't a theme park.
Most American Jews visit Israel the way other people visit Colonial Williamsburg: they want to see the past brought to life, but without having to live it themselves. When it comes to touring Israel, make and stick to a one-time tour rule: you will lead trips to Israel only for people who have not been before. After that, encourage *aliyah*: moving to Israel and becoming an Israeli citizen. But first be able to answer the question, "Why don't you make aliyah, Rabbi?"

*

Never settle for a ten-minute sermon.
If your board tells you to keep your sermons to ten minutes, tell them you will consider that when they keep their board meetings to ten minutes.

Learning takes time. If your congregants don't want to give you their time, they really don't want you to give them anything of substance at all. If your congregants get restless during your sermons, you probably need help writing better sermons. Or, possibly, you need a different congregation—or a different way of making a living.

*

Stand by your principles, not on them.
When you stand by your principles, you make judgments; when you stand on your principles, you become judgmental. When you stand by your principles, you allow and encourage others to stand by theirs.

If you are asked to violate your principles, refuse. If your board or congregants regularly ask you to violate your principles, quit.

*

Have a Plan B.
You can be fired at any time for any reason, especially if that reason just wrote a huge check to the sanctuary renovation fund. Protect yourself: have a second career even while you are pursuing your rabbinic one. That way, if your job at the synagogue goes south, you can easily move north.

*

Stop praying as if it's 1255.
If your worship services require your congregants to put aside everything they know to be true from science, sociology, history, philosophy, and their own experience, most will choose not to worship. Reinvent liturgy to reflect what we know—and to help your congregants use what they know more justly and compassionately.

*

If science disproves a teaching, drop the teaching.
If your teachings have to hide from science, chances are they are false, and you know they're false. Don't make

science into religion. Simply allow science to clear away whatever is false in your religion.

*

Don't play make believe.
Tell the truth about god. If you don't believe in the god of Abraham, Isaac, and Jacob, chances are that neither do most of your congregants. Don't pretend that god is more believable when we add Sarah, Rebecca, Leah, and Rachael to his list of followers. A dead god is a dead god, no matter how PC the eulogy. Religion is made up. Any god that can be described or conceived is made up. Tradition is made up. Torah is made up. Talmud is made up. Knowing that Judaism is made up frees you to make it up better.

*

Share what you know. Be honest about what you don't know.
Don't pretend to believe what you know to be false. Don't be afraid to talk about what you know to be true. Don't be afraid to invite others to do the same.

*

Torah! Torah! Torah!
Turning Torah is how rabbis stay spiritually alive. Make time to turn Torah every day. If the sign on your office door reads "Rabbi's Study," add one that says, "Rabbi's studying." If your board objects, saying, "Rabbi, we aren't paying you to study," what they are really saying is, "Rabbi we have no respect for you or what you are trained to do. But we are going to suck the life out of you, just the same." If and when you hear this, start making plans to leave.

*

Are you a prophet or a clerk?
A prophet challenges people to move toward teshuvah and tikkun and being a blessing to all the families of the earth (Genesis 12:3). A clerk is only interested in selling synagogue memberships. You can't be both.

If you choose to be a prophet, hire a clerk to build a strong and loving synagogue community. If you choose to be a clerk, hire a rabbi who is a prophet.

*

Your job description is "rabbi."
You're not a book or movie reviewer. You're not a political pundit. You're not an expert on the Middle East. You're not an early childhood educator. And, unless you are properly trained and licensed, you aren't a psychologist, social worker, marriage counselor, or life coach. You're a rabbi. Rabbis have only one job: teach people how to practice teshuvah and tikkun using the teachings and traditions of Judaism.

*

Don't lead, lift.
When you lead worship services, your obligation isn't to the service but to the worshipper. The goal of worship is to lift people beyond self to Self, beyond the narrow mind (mochin d'katnut) to the spacious mind (mochin d'gadlut). This is rarely done through words.

The transformative power of worship rests with silence and music. When it comes to silence, think "be still and know I am God" (Psalms 46:10) rather than mumble a prayer and move on. When it comes to music, think klezmer, Yofiyah, and Shefa Gold rather than Germanic marching songs and summer camp favorites.

*

Cantors aren't song leaders.
Cantors are shamans who are trained to use music and chant to lift people into a direct experience of God happening in, with, and as them. If your cantor can do this but hasn't been allowed to, don't waste their precious spiritual gift. If your cantor can't do this, hire a cantor who can.

*

Not every prayer is a group prayer.
Synagogue should be a place for personal and communal transformation—a place where mochin d'katnut (self and selfishness) gives way to mochin d'gadlut (Self and selflessness). This requires four things: stirring poetry, transcendent music, deep dialogue, and silent contemplation. If these aren't the building blocks of your services, you are building a Tower of Babel.

*

Speak simply enough so people can disagree.
You need to be understood. When people understand, some will disagree. Good for them; better for you. Don't hide behind jargon, technical language, or platitudes. Don't hide at all. Ever. Say what you mean, mean what you say, and be prepared to listen to those who think differently.

*

Never have the last word.
Let people react to what you say and give them time to do so. After every sermon, invite people to ask questions and offer comments. If they ask questions, answer them briefly. If they offer counter arguments, promise to consider them (and, later, do so). Clarify any misunderstandings, but don't argue your case a second time. Let your congregants have the last word. If you are concerned that this will make services too long, cut out responsive readings. No one likes them, anyway.

*

Crank it up, don't dumb it down.
When turning Torah with your community, imagine you are teaching graduate students, not preschoolers.

*

Being Jewish isn't the goal.
The goal is to be a blessing to all the families of the earth (Genesis 12:3). Being a Jew is one way to achieve the goal.

*

Don't mistake muttering in Hebrew for praying.
Just because people can pronounce the Hebrew words in a *siddur* doesn't make those words meaningful. Just because they can recite the prayers doesn't mean they are praying. Prayer is an act of transformation—of moving from narrow mind to spacious mind, from self to Self, from me to we, from taking to giving to sharing. Teach your people to pray, not just to read the script.

*

Add Jesus to your Yahrzeit list on Good Shabbat.
Don't let Christians rob us of one of the most famous Jews who ever lived. Reclaim Jesus as a first-century God-intoxicated Jewish mystic. At the very least, remember his death at the hands of Rome as you prepare to say Kaddish.

While you're at it, add Spinoza to the Yahrzeit list as well. Don't let the paranoid banning of Spinoza in 1656 rob us of one of the few Jews of the past who can still speak to Jews today. Even the Amsterdam synagogue that expelled him over three hundred and fifty years ago now celebrates him.

*

Don't try to make Judaism relevant.
Judaism—practicing teshuvah and tikkun and being a blessing to all the families of the earth (Genesis 12:3) by doing justly, acting kindly, and walking humbly (Micah 6:8)—is relevant. If you have to make "it" relevant, whatever "it" is isn't Judaism.

*

Stop stressing over the future of Jews and Judaism.
Teach the Judaism you love and do so wisely and passionately. Let the future take care of itself.

FURTHER RESOURCES

If you find the approach to Judaism expressed here intriguing and would like to know more, look into my other books on Judaism:

* *Rabbi Rami's Guide to God* (Spirituality & Health)
* *Minyan: Ten Principles for Living Life with Integrity* (Harmony Press)
* *Amazing Chesed: Living a Grace-Filled Judaism* (SkyLight Paths Publishing)
* *Open Secrets: The Letters of Reb Yerachmiel ben Yisrael* (Monkfish Book Publishing Co.)
* *The Sacred Art of Lovingkindness* (SkyLight Paths Publishing)
* *Ethics of the Sages* (SkyLight Paths Publishing)
* *Tanya, the Masterpiece of Hasidic Wisdom* (SkyLight Paths Publishing)
* *Hasidic Tales Annotated & Explained* (SkyLight Paths Publishing)

ACKNOWLEDGMENTS

This book owes its existence to my agent, Scott Edelstein. It was his idea. It is partly his title. And the first draft was his weaving together of things I had written but not published.

As much as I love to write, I love to rewrite even more. So, it was with great humility and joy that I dove into Scott's manuscript, kneading and braiding what he had collected, and adding to it as needed. This book is his and mine. Though mostly mine. Scott agrees with this.

What I don't love is editing what I write and rewrite. For this, I turn first to my friend and business partner Frank Levy, whose task it is to see if what I am doing has any value outside my own mind. Then, for a deeper dive into philosophical consistency and grammatical accuracy, I turn to my son Aaron, who is a professor of English at Middle Tennessee State University. Only when both Frank and Aaron are satisfied do I go through the manuscript one last time and send it back to Scott.

I am grateful to Scott, Frank, and Aaron for their time, effort, and devotion to making me sound smarter than I am. Though I am pretty smart. They agree with this.

I am also grateful to Paul Cohen and Monkfish Book Publishing Co. for putting their money where my mouth is. I am humbled by their faith in this project.

Thanks as well to my many mentors, teachers, and colleagues on whose shoulders I stand: Elis Rivkin, Sherwin Wine, Mordecai Kaplan, Alvin Reines, Zalman Schachter-Shalomi, Michael Lerner, Arthur Waskow, Art Green, Ellen Bernstein, Sylvia Boorstein, Jay Michaelson, David Cooper, and Alan Lew. To those among you who are still alive: I hope this book doesn't drive you toward an early grave. To those among you who are already in the grave: I hope this book doesn't drive you to turn in it.

If I've overlooked anyone who has earned my gratitude but whose name has slipped from my aging memory, my apologies. You know who you are.

ABOUT THE AUTHOR

I'm a Jew. I'm not Jew-ish.

More to the point, I am a serious Jew. As a serious Jew, I use the myths, legends, texts, and traditions of Judaism as my primary language for articulating what I experience as true about life in general, and for making meaning out the raw facts of life.

I feel lucky to be a Jew, because being a Jew encourages me to sharpen my questions rather than accept traditional answers. It urges me to value doubt over belief, and to place argument for the sake of Truth above consensus for the sake of conformity. It instills in me a love of learning, a commitment to justice and compassion, and a vow to repair the world. It calls me to be a blessing to all the families of the earth, human and otherwise.

I am an ordained Reform rabbi with a PhD in religious studies; a contributing editor for *Spirituality & Health* Magazine; a podcast host (*Spirituality & Health Podcast with Rabbi Rami*); an award-winning author of over three dozen books on religion and spirituality; and the co-founder of the One River Foundation (www.oneriverfoundation,org).

Best of all, I am a husband, father, father-in-law, grandfather, and friend.